Judge Irene H. Sullivan (ret.) is a nationally-recognized expert in juvenile and family law. She is the author of the book, *Raised by the Courts: One Judge's Insight into Juvenile Justice.* Judge Sullivan served as a family and juvenile court judge in the Tampa Bay area of Florida for 12 years. Upon her retirement, she began to teach juvenile law as an adjunct professor at Stetson University College of Law in Gulfport, Florida. She also began to serve as a guardian ad litem, appointed by the courts, in high conflict divorce and paternity cases. Judge Sullivan received the Salvation Army's Children's Justice Award in 2005, followed by awards from her local bar associations and Stetson University Law School's Hall of Fame selection. In 2022, PACE Center for Girls selected her as their advocacy champion and the Girl Scouts of West Central Florida appointed her a Woman of Distinction.

Lisa S. Negrini, Ph.D., LCSW, IMH-E brings 35 years of experience in child and family mental health, professional development, advocacy, research, workforce development and innovative initiatives for children and families. Dr. Negrini has spent her career promoting integrated community systems of care for families and developing key partnerships and collaborations across disciplines that effectively create and disseminate effective strategies and services to meet the needs of children and their families. Dr. Negrini is the Executive Director of Learning Empowered, Inc. where she works to address educational disparities for children and adults to promote healthy child development and support strong and resilient families.

Our deep appreciation to family law judges, Jack Helinger and Elizabeth Jack. Judge Helinger inspired us to write this book and then wrote his own meaningful foreword and epilogue. Judge Jack graciously shared her own personal divorce story as well as coparenting advice she gives from the bench. Judge Helinger and Jack represent the finest in family law judges. Judge Linda Allan provided advice and encouragement. Chicago judges opened their Family law courtrooms and provided advice as did Chicago guardian ad litem, Robert Ackley and attorney Bob Downs.

Thanks also to the many professionals who contributed advice on family therapy, parenting coordination, mediation, addictions, coparenting and counseling for children and families, including Dr. Wendy Coughlin, Dr. Mitchell Kroungold, Dr. Kim Costello, Dr. Eric Rosen, Dr. James McHale, Michelle Donley, LCSW, and attorneys Gay Inskeep, Joan Walker, Lee Greene, Nancy Harris, Peter Meros, Sarah Chaves, Elizabeth Burchell, Catherine Day Hult and Peggy Senentz. Thanks also to Dr. Adele Solazzo and Dr. Debra Carter. And to that wizard of word processing and friend, Jerri Evans.

Judge Irene Sullivan, Ret.
and Lisa S. Negrini, Ph.D.

You Can't Raise Children by Text

Better Coparenting in a Digital World

Austin Macauley Publishers™
LONDON * CAMBRIDGE * NEW YORK * SHARJAH

Copyright © Judge Irene Sullivan, Ret. and Lisa S. Negrini, Ph.D. 2022

The right of Judge Irene Sullivan, Ret. and Lisa S. Negrini, Ph.D. to be identified as authors of this work has been asserted by them in accordance with sections 77 and 78 of the Copyright, Designs and Patents Act 1988.

All rights reserved. No part of this publication may be reproduced, stored in a retrieval system, or transmitted in any form or by any means, electronic, mechanical, photocopying, recording, or otherwise, without the prior permission of the publishers.

Any person who commits any unauthorized act in relation to this publication may be liable to criminal prosecution and civil claims for damages.

A CIP catalogue record for this title is available from the British Library.

ISBN 9781398478619 (Paperback)
ISBN 9781398478626 (ePub e-book)

www.austinmacauley.com

First Published 2022
Austin Macauley Publishers Ltd®
1 Canada Square
Canary Wharf
London
E14 5AA

To our children of divorce

Table of Contents

Foreword	13
Introduction	15
Finding Your ACE Score	23
Part I: Real Stories – Names Changed	27
Chapter 1: When Silence Isn't Golden	29
Chapter 2: Helicopter Parents Encircling aPre-School	33
Chapter 3: Guilt, The Guilt That Texting Can't Erase	36
Chapter 4: "I Grew Up in This House, in This Room, Why Should I Leave?"	38
Chapter 5: Escalation by Text	41
Chapter 6: Casual Conceptions	44
Chapter 7: I Got What I Wanted	47
Chapter 8: Domestic Violence, Text, Text, Text and Shoot 'Em Up	50
Chapter 9: His, Hers and Theirs Times Two	54
Chapter 10: The Over Booked Child	57
Part II: The Toolbox	59
Chapter 11: Resources Used by Judges	61
Chapter 12: The Beginning: Infant Development	63
Chapter 13: Mediation	66
Chapter 14: Parent Coordination	69

Chapter 15: Family Therapy	73
Chapter 16: Coparenting Therapy	75
Chapter 17: Guardian Ad Litem	79

Part III: Difficult Cases   83

Chapter 18 Really Difficult Cases	85
Chapter 19 Mental Health and Substance Use	87
Chapter 20: He's Your Father	90
Chapter 21: Relocation	93
Chapter 22: When a Child Resists a Parent	97
Chapter 23: Who's Behind This?	102
Chapter 24: "Battle of the Therapists over Texts"	105
Chapter 25: Coparenting with A Pseudo Stranger	109
Chapter 26: Children with Different Needs	112
Chapter 27: Only Children	116
Chapter 28: What Were You Thinking?	119
Chapter 29: It's Not Equal! It's Not "Fair."	121
Bonus Chapter: Been There, Done That: "Soapbox Musings from A Family Law Judge"	125
Been There, Done That: "Soapbox Musings from a Family Law Judge"	127

Part IV: Some Solutions   141

Chapter 30: Some Practical Solutions – 10 Steps to Better Coparenting in a Digital World	143
Chapter 31: It Isn't Easy	145
Chapter 32: The Chicago Judges	149
Chapter 33: Listening	154
Chapter 34: Apologies: Why They Beat the "Damnit Doll"	159
Chapter 35: Managing Your Feelings	162

Chapter 36: Parallel Parenting	165
Part V: Collaborative Divorce	**169**
Chapter 37: What Is Collaborative Divorce?	171
Chapter 38: The Collaborative Team	173
Chapter 39: Two Lawyers Share Their Experiences	175
Chapter 40: The Mental Health Professional	177
Chapter 41: View from the Bench	179
Chapter 42: Non-Violent Communication (NVC)	180
Chapter 43: Last Words… Lighten Up… Laugh a Lot… And Love, Love, Love	183
Epilogue	**185**
Special Section: Coparenting During Covid-19 and Other Crises	**188**
Appendix, Resources	**191**
Biographies	**193**

Foreword

By: Florida Circuit Court Judge Jack Helinger

After listening to a mother and father spend most of their time testifying about negative things about the other, the family law judge paused and said to the parties, "Your hate for each other is outweighing the love for your child."

You can substitute hate with anger, animosity, jealously or any other appropriate word.

Most parents truly love their children. Then why do parents engage in this high conflict behavior that is so harmful to their children? What can be done to help them stop?

THERAPEUTIC JUSTICE The Florida Supreme Court states this should be a key part of the family court process. Therapeutic justice is a process that attempts to address the family's interrelated legal and non-legal problems to produce a result that improves the family's functioning. The process should empower families through skills development, assist them to resolve their own disputes, provide access to appropriate services, and offer a variety of dispute resolutions forums where the family can resolve problems without additional emotional trauma.

Florida, and most Family Courts throughout the country, practice Therapeutic Justice—when parents allow them. Family Courts are not like Criminal, Civil, or Probate Courts. Their goal is the best interest of children. This is best achieved by helping everyone in the family get to a better place during this incredibly difficult time.

As a family law practitioner for over 20 years and now a Family Court Judge for 13 years, I have seen the damage to children caused by parents who love them. I have tried to help parents get to a better place for their children. I have seen the parents who choose to just blame the other parent. I have also seen many parents who realize the damage they are causing their children and who want to work hard to change, effectively communicate, co-parent, and promote a great child/parent relationship with both parents.

Courts needs assistance to help these parents. Judge Irene Sullivan, retired, and Dr Lisa Negrini are two of the best. They show their knowledge, experience, passion, and love of children in these pages. They know the best way to help children is to help their parents.

Judge Irene Sullivan saw every kind of family conflict during her 12 years as a Family and Juvenile Judge. After "retirement" she now serves as a guardian ad litem (friend and spokesperson) for children. She shares observations, insight, and solutions in the following pages. I have had the honor of practicing before Judge Sullivan. She was then my colleague. She is currently helping children as a guardian ad litem in cases before me.

Dr Lisa Negrini is a psychologist who has dedicated her professional career to understanding child adversity and providing help to children, parents, and families. Her knowledge and solutions are shared in the scenarios in these pages. She has presented at numerous conferences on Adverse Childhood Experiences. We have worked together and have presented at conferences with the Courts, attorneys, psychological community and general community.

The end of a personal/romantic/marital relationship is a difficult time. But when that relationship created a precious child(ren) a parental relationship endures. Children need safety and basic necessities. But children primarily want to love and be loved by both parents. Children deserve love, security, and lack of conflict.

These stories and solutions can help anyone. Parents who love their children are in a challenging chapter of their lives. They want the best for their children and can benefit from this book. Let Judge Sullivan and Dr Negrini help your children by helping you.

Introduction

Parents love their children and want the best for them in life. That's a given. Do any parents want their children to grow up with low self-esteem, low academic performance, lack of trust, insecurity or feelings of loss and abandonment? Of course not. But that's exactly what often does happen to children in divorce and paternity cases when parents can't bury the hatchets, end the conflict and act in the best interest of their children.

Mom and dad may be divorced, re-married or living separate lives with other partners. But they are inextricably tied together with their children, even when those children become adults. A friend of mine whose parents were divorced when she was in her thirties put it this way: "My parents got rid of each other. They don't have to see each other or talk to each other. But I do. They are still my mother and my father. Now they are the grandparents of my children. I want them in my life; however, I just want them to get along."

Irene: Not everyone who reads this book has been a parent, a teacher, a therapist, a lawyer, psychologist or even a college student. Not everyone has been married, or divorced, or tried hard to co-parent. But everyone who reads this book, every adult now alive, has been a kid. The reality of having been a kid affects every area of juvenile and family law. It is the one thing that everyone relates to as they face their own family problems, their own courtrooms or therapy for the families that depend upon them.

Everyone has been a kid!

Kids are wondrous. They are fun and funny, hurting and hurtful, scared and scary and sometimes very, very brave. In my twelve years on the bench as a juvenile and family law judge, and now as a guardian ad litem in divorce and paternity cases and an adjunct professor of juvenile law, I have seen kids of every variety, size, color, intellect and disposition. They have stood before me frightened, respectful, hopeful and deceptive.

I have seen the results of domestic violence on kids. I've seen bruises and scars on arms and legs, the imprint of a hot iron on a little girl's back and the broken jaw of a mother whose son socked her in the face "because that's what all her boyfriends do to her." A 12-year-old girl whose parents were still fighting eight years after their divorce asked me in anguish: "Why can't they just get along?" A two-month-old baby whose separated parents knew each other just long enough to conceive her created a genuine moment of joy when her parents watched her "flipping over" for the first time. I felt honored to have been there with them.

In a packed courtroom one day teenager Ashley was a no show for an arraignment on her third burglary charge. When my assistant passed a phone call to me, I put it on speaker and listened to a suspiciously young voice tell me she was Ashley's mother, that Ashley was sick and couldn't make it to court. I handed the phone to Ashley's mother, who was standing before me, and the whole gallery chuckled as Ashley got a dressing down for not coming home the night before.

Then there is Toby. Toby was the bravest foster child I ever knew. I was scheduled to preside over National Adoption Day in our courthouse when Toby asked me if he could speak during the ceremony. He was 10 years old and hadn't been adopted yet so I wondered what he would say to a packed courtroom of adoptive parents, children, case workers and judges. This is the story he told:

"I was supposed to spend all day with this family who might want to adopt me. The dad picked me up and his two boys were in the back seat of the car. The dad told me to sit up front with him and he gave me a new Tampa Bay Rays baseball cap to wear. We got to their house and the mom fixed a nice lunch. I ate a lot and then me and the boys went out in the yard to play soccer. It was a lot of fun. I was starting to get hungry again and wondered what we would be having for dinner when the mom came out and told me it was time for me to go back to my foster home.

"The dad told me to sit in the back seat and he didn't say a word to me. The two boys didn't come with us. When we got to my foster home, the dad told me to give him back the baseball cap. I did and got out of the car."

There wasn't a sound in the courtroom. I knew Toby's story, but I had tears in my eyes. Then, an adoptive parent in the front row stood up and said, very loud, "Toby, those people didn't deserve you. You are too good for them."

Others began to stand and applaud the brave little boy who turned and buried his face in my black robe. (Toby was adopted a year later and is very happy.)

This is not a book about adoptions, but it is about children and how special they are. How much they deserve good co-parents if their parents don't live together. "Why can't they just get along?" I've heard that so often. Children indeed are wondrous, amazing, often challenging. Everyone should be acting in their "best interest." Above all, their parents, especially now as co-parents.

My co-author, Dr Lisa Negrini, has something important to say about Adverse Childhood Experiences.

Lisa: Feelings are universal. Children experience the same feelings as adults without the benefit of having coping skills to deal with those feelings. In lots of ways, this book is about feelings. The big feelings that children have when their parents argue, fight or have conflict. But also, the feelings that adults have about themselves as parents, their roles as protector and nurturer of their children, and the ways that they manage their relationship with their children's co-parent. This book is a reference for how parents can become more adept at dealing with their own feelings and improve the quality of the interactions that they are having with their children's co-parent.

The "why" behind this topic comes down to the fundamental feelings of children whose parents have conflict in their relationship. Children experience strong, negative feelings when their parents don't get along. Those negative feelings lead to unhealthy relationships with their parents with negative developmental consequences. We know this to be true through decades of research on adverse childhood experiences.

The original Adverse Childhood Experience Study or "ACES" was conducted in southern California between 1995 and 1997, where 17,000 adult patients were asked to complete a brief and confidential survey about their childhood experiences during an appointment for a physical. The survey took only a minute to complete and asked 10 "yes or no" questions about whether the patient had ever experienced any of the traumatic situations listed, such as parental separation or divorce, child abuse or neglect, or parental substance abuse or mental health issues. The survey was then used to determine the correlation between the trauma people experience early in life, prior to their 18th birthday, and poor health outcomes later in life. This study, conducted by Kaiser Permanente of the Center for Disease Control (CDC), turned the medical and mental health communities on their heads. It has permanently changed the way we view the connection between very negative childhood experiences and later physical and mental health outcomes.

The major finding was that the higher the incidence of adverse experiences, the higher the incidence of poor health, which only confirmed what we already believed to be true. Even more profound, however, was the discovery that poor health in most patients surveyed was not necessarily a result of their behavior, but a direct result of the trauma that was experienced in childhood. This means that if you lived through a major trauma as a young child, or experienced it over and over, your body responded as if it had experienced a physical injury. The impact to our brains and bodies when we are traumatized is recorded by the body, especially in a young, developing child. This was a profound revelation that reverberates throughout the medical and mental health communities to this day. During the following decades hundreds of studies were conducted replicating the findings from the original ACE study. We know that adversity in childhood greatly impacts a person throughout their lifespan.

For many years folks believed that a baby who witnessed violence and could not verbalize her fear or process it therapeutically simply did not recall the incident or understand it well enough to be impacted by it. The opposite is actually true. The developing brain of a young child experiences far more damage during that time of early construction than the adult brain that can call upon coping mechanisms, communicate fear, and utilize cognitive functions. Furthermore, constant exposure to negative circumstances for a young child over a period of months or years releases a flood of hormones meant to protect the body that eventually act as a poison. This is when the damage begins to occur that leads to adult illness and disease.

A broad range of research about the lifelong impact of ACEs underscores the urgency of prevention activities to protect children from adversity. When children do experience early adversity, understanding the impact of ACEs can lead to more trauma-informed interventions that help to mitigate negative outcomes. Children who experience family conflict or fighting, domestic violence, and parental separation and divorce must be supported by their families and communities. There is a strong need to effectively address and treat childhood adversity and toxic stress in order to reduce later health and social emotional problems for our children.

Divorce or separation doesn't have to cause ACEs in children. Good Coparenting can mitigate a lot. Too much emphasis on 50/50 timesharing can be as harmful as the old "custodial or visiting parent" distinction. Each case is unique. There are plenty of opportunities to connect with a child other than overnights.

Irene: Family law courts have grown up a lot in the last decade. Mental health professionals have educated judges and lawyers about the real and specific harm that children suffer when caught in the middle of a high conflict divorce or separation. The Adverse Child Experiences (ACEs) that occur to these children can have lifetime consequences, as my colleague Lisa just pointed out. No parent wants this to happen.

Trauma-informed courts have become more child centered. Judges reach into their toolbox to put resources in place to end conflict as soon as possible. The tools include early mediation, parent coordination, family therapy and guardians ad litem to be the voice of the children and to look out after their best interest. These tools work because parents surely don't want to harm their children even when they themselves are angry, fearful and distrusting of the other parent.

I saw the benefits of trauma-informed courts from the bench before I retired as a family and juvenile court judge. But it wasn't until I became a guardian ad litem that I realized up close and personal what these children experience in high conflict family law cases. As a guardian ad litem, I see the children in their homes, interacting with a parent, often that parent's partner or stepparent, and siblings. I talk to them alone in their bedrooms, surrounded by their toys, books, electronics and pets. I feel I *really* get to know them, not completely of course but much better than I did as a judge.

But, **Wait**, you say. What does this have to do with texts? The title says *You Can't Raise Children by Text*. That's why I bought the book!

Okay, patience please. Here is the connection. Just as trauma-informed, child-centered family law courts have helped high conflict parents by referring them to specific resources, technology has made things worse.

I confess. Like you I'm married to my mobile, chained to my cell, wired to my wireless, however you want to express it. It's with me all the time and I panic if I think I've lost it. It's a fun way to communicate with friends and family and to schedule appointments. You can't beat the speed and efficiency. But I'm no longer raising children.

Because of text messaging, e mail and voice messages, many co-parents raising children separately have lost the ability to really communicate—to *talk,* to *listen,* to *discuss* and maybe, just maybe, to *agree.* Not as single parents, but as co-parents who want the best for their children. Text messages, as well as e mail and voice messages, have taken the place of good Coparenting conversations. Moms and dads raising children, separately, need to talk. "Text" in the book's title, for Lisa and for me, is just a symbol of poor communication. It's that simple. That is why we wrote this book. We want to help you improve your coparenting communication.

Lisa: As we talk about the negative impact that parental conflict has on children, we want to keep the conversation framed by what we know about the impact of adverse childhood experiences (ACEs). We already know the negative effects of stress and trauma on the child's physical and mental health. Keeping these effects in mind as we discuss the ways in which children experience toxic stressors within family relationships is critical to creating an awareness of our behavior as parents and caregivers. In order to change behavior, we must first acknowledge that how we act has an impact on others. And not just any other--, the "others" who are dearest to us, whom we love and cherish the most in the world. Our children. Let's take a moment to digest and consider what we know about children who experience ACEs, and most importantly, the ACE of parental conflict, separation, and divorce.

In defining ACEs we consider childhood experiences that are stressful or traumatic events. These include: physical abuse; sexual abuse; emotional abuse; physical neglect; emotional neglect; intimate partner violence; substance misuse within household; household mental illness; parental separation or divorce or an incarcerated household member. When these events occur before age 18 there is found to be a significant relationship between the number of ACEs a person experiences and a variety of negative outcomes in adulthood, including poor physical and mental health, substance abuse, and other risky behaviors. The original Kaiser-Permanente (1997) study proved that the more ACEs a child experienced, the greater the risk for negative health outcomes.

We know that trauma has a long lasting and profound negative impact on child and adult development, health and safety. The ACE study findings suggest that negative childhood experiences are major risk factors for the leading causes of illness and death as well as poor quality of life (http://www.cdc.gov/ace/index.htm). Considering that ACEs are strongly related to the development and prevalence of a wide range of health problems for children as they emerge into adulthood, we must act now to protect our children from harmful experiences that will hurt them throughout their lives.

The harm these experiences cause is substantial. The ACE study uncovered a stunning link between childhood trauma and the chronic diseases people develop as adults, as well as social and emotional problems. This includes heart disease, lung cancer, diabetes and many autoimmune diseases, as well as depression, violence, being a victim of violence, and suicide. A broad range of research about the lifelong impact of ACEs underscores the urgency of prevention activities to protect children from these and other early traumas. When children do experience trauma, understanding the impact of ACEs can lead to more trauma-informed interventions that help to mitigate negative outcomes. It is our responsibility to effectively address and treat childhood trauma and toxic stress as we know that it will reduce significant health and social emotional problems throughout the life span.

Let us consider this as we frame our discussion about how we can do better to protect our children from the negative and toxic experiences of high conflict divorce. We can do better at making sure that our children experience healthy childhoods that will lead to healthy adulthoods full of promise and well-being.

Irene and **Lisa**: Sometimes in life things just don't go as we hoped or planned. Relationships are difficult and we are not always successful at making them work. When relationships don't work, we experience conflict and the conflict can become heavier than we can carry, unbearable. When this happens, we drift apart or run away and our response in a marriage is separation or divorce. This is a painful experience. It's painful for the adults who are experiencing it and for the family that surrounds them. The pain is especially palpable for the children who often don't understand what is going on and just know that everyone is angry, upset, scared and sad. How do we work together as the adults in our children's lives to buffer the negative impact of divorce on our children? We are going to talk about that in this book and we hope that you will join us in the journey.

Now you know a little bit about us and why we are so passionate about reducing conflict and improving coparenting. So, let's take a look at some of the situations created by text messaging and other poor communication. After that we will get to the solutions. To "what works" and the incredible tools that family law judges have in their toolbox to improve coparenting.

To keep things simple, we have chosen to use the word "child" in place of "children" and "divorce" even in paternity situations where the parents aren't married. We've chosen "coparenting" to emphasize a joint effort, rather than single parents raising a child. Our emphasis always is on the best interest of the child.

Let's begin the journey to better coparenting.

Finding Your ACE Score

While you were growing up, during your first 18 years of life:

1. Did a parent or other adult in the household **often**
Swear at you, insult you, put you down, or humiliate you?

Or

Act in a way that made you afraid that you might be physically hurt?
Yes No

If yes enter 1_____

2. Did a parent or other adult in the household **often** … Push, grab, slap, or throw something at you?

Or

Ever hit you so hard that you had marks or were injured?
Yes No

If yes enter 1_____

3. Did an adult or person at least 5 years older than you ever…
Touch or fondle you or have you touch their body in a sexual way?

Or

Try to or actually have oral, anal, or vaginal sex with you?
Yes No

If yes enter 1_____

4. Did you **often** feel that …
No one in your family loved you or thought you were important or special?

Or

Your family didn't look out for each other, feel close to each other, or support each other?
Yes No

If yes enter 1_____

5. Did you **often** feel that …
You didn't have enough to eat, had to wear dirty clothes, and had no one to protect you?

Or

Your parents were too drunk or high to take care of you or take you to the doctor if you needed it?
Yes No

If yes enter 1_____

6. Were your parents **ever** separated or divorced?
Yes No

If yes enter 1_____

7. Was your mother or stepmother:
Often pushed, grabbed, slapped, or had something thrown at her?

Or

Sometimes or often kicked, bitten, hit with a fist, or hit with something hard?

Or

Ever repeatedly hit over at least a few minutes or threatened with a gun or knife?

Yes No

If yes enter 1_____

8. Did you live with anyone who was a problem drinker or alcoholic or who used street drugs?

Yes No

If yes enter 1_____

9. Was a household member depressed or mentally ill or did a household member attempt suicide?

Yes No

If yes enter 1_____

10. Did a household member go to prison?
Yes No

If yes enter 1_____

Now add up your "Yes" answers:_____ **This is your ACE Score**

Part I
Real Stories – Names Changed

Chapter 1
When Silence Isn't Golden

What Infants and Toddlers Learn About Life When Their Parents Don't Speak To Each Other

Irene: Marilee and Tony didn't trust online dating, so they met through a mutual friend and their first date was at a trendy downtown restaurant. They found they liked the same kind of craft beers and fried calamari appetizers, so they got off to a good start. Tony chose the wine for their dinner of steamed shrimp, coleslaw, and key lime pie. Marilee beamed as he held his credit card out for the bill. What a match, she thought. Although the conversation had been light, their vibes seemed right.

So right that when Tony suggested a nightcap at his apartment, Marilee tossed away her better judgment. One sip of scotch led to another. Before she thought again, she and Tony were in bed together, and neither thought to ask about protection.

Two nights later, on their second date at a wine bar, they traded life stories which ended in a loud argument as both Merilee and Tony felt deceived. It turned out that Tony was still married, although separated, and he had just broken up with a long-time girlfriend from work. On the other hand, Marilee had represented herself as a newspaper reporter, although she had just been let go as a result of the newspaper's downsizing. Marilee and Tony agreed that those initial deceptions had torpedoed their relationship, so they said goodbye. Both twenty-five years old and college educated, they knew that life held other encounters for them.

Two months later, Marilee's gynaecologist confirmed what the test kit had revealed. She was pregnant! It could only be Tony's child. Marilee found her old text message and told Tony, "You're a dad." She had to admit she was excited, and she was sure that Tony could care less. She had other friends who were single moms. She didn't need Tony's child support, as her new job in city government paid well with benefits. She could raise this child on her own.

Tony was thrilled. Neither his wife nor his last girlfriend wanted children. He couldn't believe his luck! He had nieces and nephews and friends with young children. He couldn't wait to join them. He didn't need a wife or a girlfriend. He could raise this child on his own.

Two years later they are still before a family court judge trying to work out time sharing problems. Their little boy, Thomas, was 1 ½ years old. Marilee believes that she is the primary parent. Tony can see him on some weekends, she says, but that is all, and she needs his child support payments. I'm her equal, Tony says, and I love and want Thomas in my life at least 50% of the time or more. I'm his father, after all. Tony suggests his mother, who always wanted a grandchild, can help with the childcare. Marilee, horrified, says she has never met his family, and that she can provide care by choosing a good day care site.

Two strangers having sex. Result is one baby boy whose parents are still strangers and do not like or trust each other.

Thomas is now 18 months old. By Court order, he has gone back and forth between Marilee and Tony on a schedule that was increased when she ceased nursing Thomas. Marilee and Tony are no longer just strangers to each other. It is fair to say that they "hate" each other for wanting to share their son's life. They are in court continuously with small problems and unrealistic ideas to omit the other parent. Marilee's position hasn't changed: many of her friends are single moms, she can be too, and she resents a "stranger's" involvement. Tony's response is that this is the best thing that has happened to him. He's always wanted to be a father and Thomas is the joy of his life, even though he never wishes to see or talk to Marilee ever again. He got his wish. Tony and Marilee only communicate by text messages.

A week later, at a court-ordered 6 p.m. exchange of Thomas at a supermarket parking lot, Tony arrives early as usual and Marilee—usually late—arrives a bit early too, with Thomas in at car seat behind her. Tony is excited and walks over to the car to wave at Thomas, who waves back and smiles at Tony, a father he knows and loves. Tony looks to Marilee who points at her watch, raises her hand and mouths "five minutes." Tony looks confused so Marilee sends him a text that says: "Five minutes. Exchange to start at six." Meanwhile, Thomas looks at Tony through the glass window, claps his hands, raises his fists trying to hit the window.

The scream that breaks the silence comes from Thomas as he struggles to get to his father's welcoming arms while his mother counts the seconds and minutes until six o'clock.

Lisa: The Exchange: The scream, Thomas's scream, is a sign of his distress at this transitional moment. It is the signal that Thomas is feeling the emotional pull of his parents' conflict and he doesn't know how to manage it. What is Thomas trying to tell us with his scream? Maybe that he feels the tension in the car, that he wants to see his Daddy, or that he doesn't understand what is happening right now. Most certainly that he is distressed with this situation and he is desperate for it to be resolved.

At 18 months old, Thomas has grown to love and want each of his parents. By this age, Thomas has had the opportunity to become attached and connected to both of his parents in separate and distinct ways. Each of his parents loves and adores him, cares for him, and is eager to be bonded to Thomas and to parent well. Marilee and Tony agree on one thing: that Thomas is the center of their world and he is to be loved, nurtured, and protected. What they don't agree on is how to do this, how to share, how to co-parent. What they don't realize is that their conflict over Thomas's care is hurting Thomas in profound and long-lasting ways.

From conception, babies experience their parents' emotions. Throughout pregnancy, babies experience their mother's emotions through the rhythm of her heartbeat, the sound of her vocal cords, and the release of hormones that signal calm (endorphins) or distress (cortisol). Babies are capable of experiencing, hearing and feeling the world around them, and know how their parents are feeling. If parents are happy and peaceful, baby feels this. If parents are stressed and anxious, baby knows. Babies sense parent feelings and state of mind, and more importantly, babies are experiencing these feelings, good or bad, with their parents.

If babies are experiencing their parent's feelings in utero, then we can easily translate our understanding of how newborns and developing young children absorb their parents' feelings when they begin to live life in relationships with their parents, family members and others.

Thomas is trying to communicate his distress in this moment of exchange by screaming, trying to reach out to his father and waving his fists in anger. His confusion and frustration are apparent, and he is doing his best to let his parents know that he is upset. Since he doesn't have the words yet to express himself, he will use the ways that he knows to make his feelings known; scream, cry, hit and become emotionally dysregulated. This moment is painful for Thomas and he wants his parents to know. But what Thomas's parents don't know is that this moment of intense distress, which has been preceded by countless other moments just like this and will likely be followed by countless more in the future, is profoundly and catastrophically changing the ways that Thomas's brain functions, how he regulates and expresses his feelings and how he will be in relationships with others throughout his life.

Chapter 2
Helicopter Parents Encircling aPre-School

Irene: When Tiffany and Buddy broke up, they both thought they were mature and intelligent enough to co-parent their four-year old son Dexter rationally, keeping their emotions in check and acting in Dexter's "best interest," something they learned in the mandatory Children and Divorce Course. As each had college degrees and worked in the high-tech industry, they agreed to use e mail and text messages to communicate about Dexter.

Six months after the divorce their amicable agreement fell apart, over the choice of a pre-kindergarten for Dexter. While they both vigorously agreed on the value of early learning, Tiffany and Buddy had very different ideas of what a pre-K should look like for Dexter. Tiffany wanted a Montessori-type school where Dexter had freedom to explore, learn on his own and express his creativity. Buddy was adamant that Dexter should attend the tuition-free pre-K at his zoned school where he would be enrolled in kindergarten the next year. Buddy said he should begin to mix with children from all income levels and learn to abide by the rules set by the teachers.

Dexter was extremely bright and had adjusted well to fifty/fifty time sharing with his parents. However, he was curious and excited about school and he wanted to know where he would be going for pre-K. After all, his parents had talked about it for years and he had friends in his play group, at church and in his neighborhood, who were already in pre-K. At age four, he was used to being "enrolled" as he played mini soccer, went to Bible class on Sundays and took art lessons at Creative Clay. He just wanted to know where he would start school, begging each parent to tell him and aware, even at four years old, of their conflict.

Tiffany and Buddy began their battle on email and then resorted to text messages because "it was quicker," she said, and "she reads it right away," he said. They were so entrenched in their positions that they alone knew what was in Dexter's "best interest" that they paid no attention to the other's opinions. Although not wanting to put Dexter in the middle, they began to curse or read portions of text messages aloud in front of him. Never once did they sit down together to discuss the matter and go over the literature and/or ratings for each school. Never once did either suggest that they visit the schools together or take Dexter with them to the schools. They never had even a phone conversation about the issue.

Dexter became confused and discouraged. One week during his time-sharing exchange he said to both of them that he no longer wanted to go to school. He began to act out and broke some clay pots in his art class.

Lisa: What is happening to Dexter as he watches his parents argue over his school? We often don't consider the tension, distress and unhappiness that even very young children sense between their parents. Dexter knows that his parents are having negative feelings towards each other and he knows that it is about him. What do you think this four-year-old is thinking about the cause and effect in this situation? In case you didn't draw the connections here, let's talk about it.

Children blame themselves for their parent's conflict. At four years old, Dexter is still in a very ego-centric developmental period where he believes that things happen because of him. Dexter feels responsible for the conflict that his parents are having about his school because it is about him. With this feeling of responsibility comes a range of negative feelings about himself. He believes that he is the cause of bad things, that he is bad and that he is the reason others are unhappy. This leaves Dexter feeling guilty, ashamed, and angry at himself for being the cause of the problem. I wonder, do Dexter's parents understand just how damaging this conflict is for Dexter's developing sense of self? He is only four years old, yet he is adopting a view of himself as a problem. He is not yet old enough to understand that his parents are to blame for the conflict that they have. He believes he is responsible. Dexter has a new personal narrative that sounds like this in his head, "My parents are mad because of me, it's my fault that they are fighting and that they don't like each other. I am bad because I cause lots of problems. I am mad and sad."

When young children in high conflict custody situations begin to understand the feelings of their parents, they frequently blame themselves for their parent's feelings, good or bad. This is a part of the ego-centric developmental phase that they are in. When children blame themselves for adult conflict they carry the burden of the guilt and shame but also a piece of the anger and pain. Dexter is already experiencing angry outbursts because he doesn't have the ability to understand or talk about his feelings. He is just a small child who is carrying the weight of adult problems on his shoulders.

What should his parents be doing? At four years old, children need to have decisions made for them without their input. Young children are just trying to figure out how the world works and shouldn't be burdened with adult decisions. Ultimately, Dexter doesn't care where he goes to Pre-K, he just wants everyone to agree and be happy. Certainly, his parents should consider this and begin to have in-person or phone discussions about the Pre-K choices, including visits to each school. Do this for Dexter!

Chapter 3
Guilt, The Guilt That Texting Can't Erase

Irene: "I feel guilty about telling my Dad that I had a good time on vacation with my mom. I'm afraid I'll hurt his feelings," Emily, a thin, blonde 11-year-old told me while a tear ran down her cheek.

As a juvenile judge, I was used to seeing guilt in Court and in fact I liked it when kids showed guilt or remorse for their delinquent acts. It was the first step towards rehabilitation, which is the goal of juvenile court. But for an innocent child caught in the middle between divorced and angry parents, to feel guilty for something that isn't her fault? That is very sad and harmful.

I asked Emily how the vacation had begun. How had her parents arranged for her to go on vacation with her mother?

"They never talk, they always send text messages to each other. My dad drove me to the parking lot as usual on a Friday night. My mom wasn't there, and he swore to himself and started texting her again and again. About ten minutes later she pulled up next to us, rolled down her window and shouted "Asshole." Then I saw her fingers typing a text on her phone. I got out of the car and grabbed my suitcase from the back seat. My dad was still texting on his phone and I could tell it made my mom angry as she threw her phone on the floor and gave him the finger, shot him a bird. As soon as I got in her car, my dad peeled off at a high speed, the tires screeching. I didn't get to say goodbye to him. A few days later he called on my phone to ask me if any of my mother's friends were with us at Hilton Head. He didn't want to talk about much else."

Guilt. What a burden precious Emily is carrying that even a nice vacation with her mom is spoiled by unnecessary, angry text exchanges.

Just imagine the difference it would have made to Emily if she heard her parents talking in person or on the phone, about the vacation. What they would be doing? Who they would be seeing? How often would Emily call him? Just imagine the difference it would have made to Emily if her dad had taken her suitcase over to her mom's car, exchanging small talk with the mom and smiling, then giving Emily a big hug and kiss and telling her to "have a great time on vacation with mom. I'll talk to you soon." A warm hand off, we call it in Court. For Emily, all the difference in the world.

Lisa: No matter what their age, children experience profound guilt when they feel responsible for their parent's conflict. Emily is experiencing guilt and shame about enjoying one parent at a time. Think about what Emily's parents have loaded onto her narrow shoulders already. The loss of and hope for her mom and dad to be together with her as a family, the carefree joy that children should feel when they are with their parents, learning about communication and problem solving from her two most important role models, being able to express the joy she has when she has fun experiences with either parent, and being a child. Now Emily must also carry the burden of guilt that she feels for having the conflict between them feel like her fault.

Chapter 4
"I Grew Up in This House, in This Room, Why Should I Leave?"

Irene: Valerie and Russell were high school sweethearts. They and all their friends knew that they would be married soon after high school and have two perfect kids—a boy and a girl. They did that, as well as working hard to put each other through college, holding part and full-time jobs and spending most of their spare time and money in family activities.

Maybe it at all happened too soon, when they were too young, for as time passed and their children, Russell Jr and Francis, became teenagers, their parents grew apart, forming different friends, different interests and a growing feeling of disrespect, approaching loathing, for each other. In the last two years they began to communicate mostly by text, even when together or in their separate bedrooms. They began going out separately at night, to country music bars and social events. Russell quickly got a girlfriend and sent Valerie a text suggesting they each date other people, while staying married for the kids' sake. Valerie was shocked at first. Indeed, she *was* interested in Gary, a single man at her workplace, but she still considered herself a married woman although she and Russell rarely spoke. But she agreed to Russell's scheme and began dating Gary, recently divorced and ten years older.

Russell Jr and Francis, now in high school, suspected what was going on but as long as there were no loud arguments in front of them, the refrigerator was full and their school and sports needs were paid for, they frankly didn't care. Russell Jr had his driver's license, so they had wheels to get around. Their lives hadn't changed much—that is until their mother moved out of the family home and into Gary's apartment. She wanted a divorce and for the children to spend half their time with her and Gary. Used to using text messages to avoid difficult conversations, she sent each child a text message suggesting a 50/50 time sharing schedule with their father, week on and week off. Their father left the decision up to them, as he was having too good a time dating a few women from a strip club. Frankly, having the kids out of the house every other week was fine with him.

Russell Jr agreed to the time sharing as he wasn't really attached to his bedroom and it was an excuse to drive more often, as his mother supplied gas money. Both kids liked mom's boyfriend Gary, but Francis vehemently refused to spend any overnights at his apartment because she was "totally settled in my room with my computer, printer, TV, music system, swimming medals, stuffed animals, pictures of family and friends and all my clothes." She texted this to her mother, ending "I'm not going to put my stuff in a backpack and go back and forth. I'm just not going to do it. I grew up in this house, in this room. Why should I leave?"

Valerie was hurt by this response, but somewhat understanding. She replied by text that they could keep in touch that way, and perhaps meet once a week for breakfast, lunch or dinner. She said she would continue to go to swimming meets and school events. Francis answered curtly, "Fine."

As this family unit broke up, without a lot of overt conflict, changes were made so swiftly without any real discussion or communication. Will this have a dramatic impact on the lives of these teenagers as they grow into adults. What can we expect?

Lisa: Adolescence is a difficult time in the life span of a child. Their growing brains and bodies are in a state of rapid change. Although they still want and need their parents, it is developmentally appropriate for them to move towards independence. Adolescents are still centered on their own thoughts and desires and sometimes have difficulty considering the impact of their decisions on others and on their own future. They are heavily influenced by their peers and by their pursuit of their own justice.

Russell Jr and Francis may be more concerned with how their parents' divorce affects their current lives and day to day functioning than they are about anything else. They may be striving to maintain the normalcy that they have always known and push back on change that feels scary and cumbersome to them. This thinking is appropriate for teens as this is the time when they are planning how they will navigate the world independently from their parents. The impact that a divorce has on the family, on their parents and on the other sibling may not be in the front of their minds. If those thoughts creep in occasionally,

Russell Jr and Francis may push those thoughts out because they are too difficult to think about and to feel. It is easier to not think about a divorce or feel it than it is to deal with it. Teens will take the easy route here as talking about, processing and expressing emotions are not usually a teen's most solid skill set.

We must consider what will happen if the thoughts and feelings associated with their parents' divorce are not discussed. We all know that the bottling up of feelings is not healthy. When we suppress unwanted feelings, we end up paying the price later. We pay that price not only emotionally but also in our physiology with digestive problems, headaches, high blood pressure, heart disease and an assortment of other physical ailments. These ailments are our bodies responses to toxic stress. Like all ACEs, divorce has a lasting impact on our mind and bodies, and on our mental and physical health.

Of all of the reasons that divorce impacts children's and teen's physical and emotional health, the deterioration of the child-parent relationship may be the most important. Teens still need their parents' love, support, guidance, and limit setting. Although teens may look like grownups, they are still children with strong emotional needs for connection, parenting, and family. When parents divorce, the child-parent relationships within the family often become strained with one parent or both parents. This relationship strain puts incredible stress on children and their development. This strain can lead to parent alienation, parent-child conflict, and irreparable relationship injury.

Russell Jr and Francis both need to feel the support and love of both of their parents. Although Valerie and Russell should consider their teen's choices about their living situations, they should make a strong effort to stay connected, spend meaningful time with them and be engaged in the lives of their teens. Even though teens pretend to not need their parents, this is not the fact. They need them more than ever.

If we are to help teens become happy healthy adults, it is imperative that we stay close to them in many ways. This means talking often in person, giving them the chance to express themselves, respecting their growing needs for independence, providing opportunities to discuss important issues, spending quality time together, and fostering positive relationships. Our teens rely on their parents to ease family transitions with love, kindness and connection.

Chapter 5
Escalation by Text

Irene: The family law judge asked the divorced parents how they communicated with each other during their conflict over their 13-year-old son's summer vacation. Both parents were wealthy. Dad wanted the boy to spend the summer at his mountain home in Colorado. Mom had arranged a European tour, connected to her publishing business.

They wouldn't look at each other. Neither spoke. The judge asked again, "How do you two talk to each about the issue?"

"By text," the mom said.

"Yes," the dad agreed, producing a thick packet of screenshots. "And I have the proof here of copies of her text messages to show they are nothing but a constant rant of blather, fear, profanity and nonsense. No straight answers to my demands."

"His demands are just that, threatening me, your honor," the mom tearfully replied. "I've saved them on my phone to show you." She rose from her seat, but her lawyer motioned her to sit back. "It's like he's shouting at me. I start to shake when I read them. My doctor prescribed pills and I…"

"Drug addict, your honor," the dad snorted. "Just read these tests and you'll see she is woozy, can't complete a sentence or thought and she's…" His attorney shut him up.

"That's why I blocked him from my phone, Judge," the mom said openly, weeping. "I can't stand his messages. And I've already purchased airline and hotel reservations all throughout Europe. I've arranged for my mother to babysit my one-year-old child."

"She did that without getting permission from me. My son has *always* spent summers in Colorado…"

"That's when we were still married…" she interrupted.

"She can't change it now. Look at these messages, Judge." The dad tried hard to shove the copies towards the judge at the end of the table.

"Whoa," the judge said, holding up both hands. "Did either of you speak to the other about this dispute, by phone or in person?"

Neither parent spoke.

"Did either of you speak to your son about what he wants during this vacation?"

"I know what he wants," both parents blurted out simultaneously.

That was my signal to stand.

"Judge, I'm the guardian ad litem assigned by the court for this young man. I have spoken to him three times, at both parents' house and at school. The boy is distraught, to the point of tears, over this argument between his parents. He loves them both, but each of them has forwarded to him many of these text messages that you've seen. He told me that reading them makes him feel sick. He loves his mom and he loves his dad. He hates that they cuss at each other.

"No one has asked his opinion, but I am the guardian ad litem assigned to the case and I have opinions about what the child wants. This summer he wants to stay home, attend scout camp for his Eagle Badge, and enjoy his new baby brother. That's his honest wish, your honor?"

Lisa: Visualize a child holding two ropes and their parents playing tug of war with the child in the middle, angrily pulling, yelling, not conscious of the pain that is being inflicted on the child, only thinking of their own need to win, to have it their way, to be the victor. The children racked with pain, tears streaming down their face, begging for their parents to stop pulling them apart. The tortured child wanting the pain to stop, only wanting to have everyone step back and stop hurting each other. Nowhere to hide, nowhere to turn, no one to talk to. Enter the guardian ad litem.

A child's voice is heard by the guardian ad litem. The guardian holds the child's pain, their fears, and their needs. The child finally has a voice that can be heard, a protector and advocate. Through the guardian, the child speaks and asks that their parents pay attention to what they need. The burden of this ask is on the child and the guardian. We hear the child's voice echo "help me, protect me, save me", a voice that is full of pain and sadness.

Thankfully our system allows for a guardian to speak for the child, to remind the parents that their child is a human being in formation, striving for maturation and full of needs, fears and hope. There is a bit of irony here. That a non-family member should need to enter the family system to protect the children and ensure their voice is heard and that they are safe. Isn't this the parents' job? Aren't the parents responsible for making sure that no one is hurting their child? What is our expectation that parents keep children safe from emotional abuse, from distress, from the pain that can only be inflicted by those that we love and need the most? Perhaps these rhetorical questions should be answered by parents as we attempt to illuminate the impact of their behavior on their children. Perhaps we should remind parents of what happens if they don't consider their behavior on their child's health and well-being.

I will forecast the life experiences of this 13-year-old boy if his parents don't figure out how to co-parent him with less conflict. He is already experiencing acute distress. He suffers from moments of sadness, anger, humiliation, and grief. These moments turn into depression and anxiety as he struggles to manage the heavy weight of his parent's triangulation of him and their constant aggression towards one another. His anger and aggression become overwhelming for him and he begins to emotionally pull away from both parents. He becomes quiet, socially withdraws and begins to fail academically. He loses friends, starts getting into trouble because of angry outbursts and gets suspended from school. The fighting between his parents gets worse because they now blame each other for their child's struggles. He retreats further and begins to self-medicate, sneaking alcohol from the liquor cabinet and buying beer from kids in the street. By next year, he is on the edge of being expelled from school, being arrested for juvenile offenses and is establishing serious patterns of substance use and unstable mental health. He is a now a teenager in trouble and his parents can no longer reach him. They have done too much damage and the attempts at repair are too little, too late. A challenging and perhaps impossibly difficult life course has been set for him by the parents who were supposed to protect him.

It all slips away so fast. Our children are only young for the blink of an eye and then they must lead their lives with the foundations that we build for them. What kind of foundation are you building for your child? What type of future are you setting them up for? Will you put your child's future before your own feelings and work diligently to co-parent in ways that support your child's health and well-being? Child-centered means considering your child above all else, it does not mean getting out the tug a war rope.

Chapter 6
Casual Conceptions

Irene: In the ten years I have been serving as a guardian ad litem, I have met dozens of children who have been "casually conceived," meaning their parents were never married or even partners. Their parents never lived together, nor were in a committed relationship. It wasn't a one-night stand. There were a few dates, but never a big breakup, as neither parent had much invested. Yet, they had sex, and had a child together. And now, in addition to all the other children, former spouses, in laws and step-children in their lives, these parents will be connected for their lives through this child, and his education, his adulthood, his marriage(s) and probably their grandchildren. If I can extrapolate from the dozens of "casually conceived" children in my cases to the whole population, there must be thousands and thousands of these children who rotate from mom to dad every few days, without ever having lived together as a family.

Single parents Robin and Josh met on a soccer field where their six-year-old sons played on the same team. They chatted on the side lines during practice and cheered together in the stands at game time. The boys had a few play dates at each other's home, and Josh invited Robin to a movie and drinks afterwards. She cooked dinner for him one night, followed by sex. He reciprocated, followed by sex. They continued to see other people—nothing serious. Josh was habitually late, which annoyed Robin. She was always short of cash, which annoyed Josh. Although their sons were still best buddies, Robin and Josh lost interest in each other. Then Robin learned that she was pregnant. She didn't tell Josh until she found out the baby was a girl. They both want this little girl—they just don't want each other.

Coparenting between Robin and Josh is like a business relationship, and the parenting plan a contract. They aren't even good friends, much less lovers or spouses. On one hand, there was no betrayal, no emotional break up or bitter divorce. On the other hand, they haven't developed the trust between them which is essential for good coparenting. They don't know each other well enough to trust each other with someone as fragile and helpless as a new baby. Their new baby!

A good parent coordinator or therapist would work with Robin and Josh during the pregnancy. They both could express their desires and doubts, fears and frustrations in a neutral, professional setting and get valuable advice. Parenting plans could be drafted for different stages of the child's first few years. More timesharing for mom with a newborn, gradual overnights for dad if breast milk is pumped or formula used. Robin and Josh could attend together a class for parents of newborns. They could walk through each other's homes looking for hazards. Their sons could be brought into the picture, probably delighted at the prospect of a baby sister as well as another connection between them.

There are a lot of positives in this relationship. Mainly the absence of negatives! The child hasn't witnessed major arguments, yelling and screaming or physical abuse. The child doesn't have memories of her parents being together, so there's not that feeling of loss. Essentially, the child is growing up with two distinct parents, homes, and extended families. Of course, it is much easier if the parents live close to each other and to the child's school.

Let's hope that Robin and Josh treat coparenting like a healthy business relationship, including the calculation of child support. That they honor and respect the other's concerns and share information about the child. That they plan occasional outings together with their baby and their boys. Then this little girl could grow up well-adjusted and very happy with two loving parents whose most important connection to each other was to conceive her.

Lisa: Many babies and children have parents that don't live together, never cohabitated, and don't know each other very well. For many of those children, being raised by co-parents is a wonderful experience and the children grow up knowing that they are loved and cared about by many people. Robin and Josh could start out on the right foot, with good intentions, and hope that they will work out their coparenting in the best interest of their daughter. Staying child-centered in coparenting is critical. In order to do that, co-parents must be able to manage their own feelings and come to communication about their child in cooperative and collaborative ways. If Robin and Josh establish an intentionally helpful communication style early in their coparenting relationship, they have a great chance of ensuring that their beautiful daughter will flourish in their shared relationships.

Robin and Josh may want to start off their communication about what their new daughter needs in her earliest days and weeks. We know that infancy is a critical developmental time period. Newborn babies are experiencing rapid brain development and trust in their relationships, environments and world. During the early months of life, infants need to experience as much consistency and predictability as possible. This means that their environments, routines and, most especially, their caregivers, need to be a steady presence in their lives. Knowing what we know about what infants need, how do we determine the healthiest ways for both mothers and fathers to experience the joys, connection and bonding that happen with their infants in those earliest days and months? This is an important conversation for Robin and Josh to be having during their daughter's infancy.

Robin and Josh can be considering and discussing their daughter's need to develop and maintain regular routines for sleeping, waking, eating and interaction time. Infants need to have frequent contact and interaction with both parents and all caregivers that will be important in the infant's life. Because infants are changing and growing rapidly, co-parents need to communicate about the infant's development, and maintain some flexibility to adjust to the infant's needs.

The communication that Robin and Josh and all co-parents have regarding their baby's needs is incredibly important. Not just because of the rapid development of the baby but also because of the innate sensitivity that infants are born with. Starting at a very early age, babies can sense and feel fear as well as recognize anger and harsh words. Communicating for calm is critical for baby's developing sense of trust and safety. Reducing any conflict in the relationship and improving communication should begin as soon as co-parents decide that they are going to co-parent together. If begun with positive intention, kindness and determination, Robin and Josh can have a successful coparenting relationship that stays collaborative, cooperative and child centered.

Chapter 7
I Got What I Wanted

Irene: Todd and Christi met through sporting goods. They were both athletes in high school and college. Todd worked at a large sporting goods chain store in a big city, on track to become manager soon. Christi worked in sales for a line of golfing and tennis equipment. She regularly visited Todd on business.

It wasn't surprising, then, when Todd and Christi began dating. Their interests in sports and sport business seemed to make them compatible. After exchanging numerous text messages and a month of dating, Christi moved into Todd's two-bedroom apartment and it seemed to Todd that their relationship could become permanent. Soon they began to argue. Todd thought Christi lacked "intimacy." Although their sex life was great, she didn't seem to want to hug or kiss him or even show that she was happy to be with him. She didn't introduce him to many of her friends. On the other hand, Christi thought Todd was trying to "control my emotions." She told me: "I grew up shuttled between relatives, without a real parent. I don't want Todd to tell me how I should feel about him."

Todd and Christi discussed their problems, sometimes by text. They had enjoyable times together, especially when playing golf or biking, but Todd continued to think that Christi didn't value him, didn't really love him as he did her. They decided that having a child might bring them closer together. They stopped using protection, and lo and behold Christi quickly became pregnant.

A few months later they learned their child was a boy. Two months after that Christi withdrew from all forms of intimacy. Seven months pregnant, she moved out of Todd's apartment saying it was over and that she would send him a text when she went into labor.

Todd was present during the birth. He held his son high in both hands, with his own mother present. They had agreed to name their son Tiger, after the great golfer. However, Todd never saw the birth certificate and never learned until later that he wasn't listed as father.

Todd had to beg Christi to see Tiger. Nothing had been legally established, so he saw Tiger when Christi allowed him to, by sending Todd a text. Christi let Todd hold him, feed him, and diaper him at those times, but they only lasted two to three hours, once a month. When Todd said he wanted more time, and to be legally designated Tiger's father, Christi refused. Todd thought he was going to have to hire a lawyer, but Christi beat him to it. At the next visit with his son, she brought an agreement, prepared by her lawyer, asking him to sign it. While it acknowledged that Todd was Tiger's biological father, it contained a provision whereby Todd would relinquish all rights to Tiger, with no obligation for child support and no time sharing other than as allowed by Christi, a minimum of once a month, to be arranged by text messages, which were to be their only form of communication.

Todd was shocked, upset and unwilling at first to sign the agreement. However, Christi told Todd she had secretly recorded on her cell phone some admissions he had made regarding taking home some sports items such as golf clubs, bags and tennis rackets which were on sale, for his personal use, without notifying his boss. Todd kept a list of such equipment so that he could prove they were all sales items that no one seemed to want. Christi had taken a screen shot of that list and threatened to go to Todd's boss if he didn't sign the agreement. I could be fired for this, Todd thought, and reluctantly signed the agreement.

For the last three years Todd's only contact with his son has been at Christi's discretion, for about two hours once a month. When he asked to be called "daddy," Christi sent him a text saying that he's not a real "daddy" and that name would be reserved for a man Christi hoped she would eventually marry.

When Todd got angry and sent Christi a text questioning her motives during their entire relationship, Christi sent a text with a smiling emoji followed by "I got what I wanted."

How confusing is it for Tiger now and as he gets older? What is the harm done to the child, which neither parent really acknowledges?

Lisa: Children all have two parents. This is not only a fact, it's apparent to all children as they grow and learn how babies are made. They also become aware of the fact that many other children have a Mom and a Dad. If they only have one parent in their lives, they will need to know why. Children are naturally inquisitive about this part of their lives and sensitive about it as well. In addition to the ways that "families" are portrayed in the media, children understand the broader community and the contributions that both moms and dads and other co-parents play in the lives of children.

Tiger has had the chance to get to know his father. He has begun a relationship with Dad and he will want to continue that relationship. No matter who comes into Christi's life in the future, Todd will always be Tiger's father. Children have room for multiple coparenting adults in their lives. Mom, dad, uncles, aunts, grandparents, boyfriends and girlfriends. Children need relationships, connection and love from everyone.

Tiger has a lot to lose if Todd's role in his life is limited. Fathers provide nurturing, structure, resources, emotional support, extended family, a sense of community, discipline, and so much more to their children's lives that it is not even possible to state it all here. Not only would Todd lose out on the joy of a relationship with his son, but Tiger would miss out on so many things if Todd was not in his life. Perhaps Christi will reconsider how vital the relationship between Tiger and Todd is to Tiger's growth and development as well as his future.

Chapter 8
Domestic Violence,
Text, Text, Text and Shoot 'Em Up

Irene: Fred was not happy that his timesharing with his only child, Stephanie, was cut short. However, when he and Stephanie's mother, Connie, were divorced they agreed in writing that Stephanie would spend each parent's birthday with that parent. This Sunday was Connie's 35th birthday. Thirteen-year-old Stephanie held her mother's present in her lap as Fred slowed down outside Connie's house.

"Shit!" Fred yelled, pointing to a black SUV parked at the curb. "That's her damn boyfriend's car. She said she broke up with him. He's a real bad guy. I don't like him and you shouldn't be around him." Fred sent a text to Connie: "Get the SOB out. Stephanie can't come 'til he leaves. Have gun. Will use." Fred reached over Stephanie and pulled a revolver out of the glove compartment. Stephanie screamed and sent a text to her mother on her own phone. "He's got a gun. Acting crazy." Connie sent a text reply: "Just run to the house. He won't shoot you." Stephanie ran towards the house as her mother opened the door, shotgun in hand. Stephanie screamed, "Don't shoot dad." Connie's boyfriend Jim pushed Stephanie aside and ran towards the car. *Ping!* It was the last thing Fred heard before Jim grabbed Fred's revolver and began to choke him. Connie's text read "F U, U Jerk."

Where was a phone call? A conversation? A call to law enforcement? Nothing but text messages and Stephanie's screams. There is obviously a lot more going on between Connie and Fred than just text messaging, but it is symptomatic of their problems.

Lisa: Children living in a home rattled by domestic violence suffer in many ways. That alone is a reason to end the toxic relationship, be it a marriage or a live-in situation. However, sometimes domestic violence continues in one form or another after a separation and poisons the post-divorce relationship. Power and control issues remain, even when physical injuries end. Children are hyper vigilant and sensitive to domestic violence even when their parents are separated. It cannot be ignored; rather, it must be dealt with.

The age of the child significantly affects a child's actions and reactions when they have been exposed to domestic violence. A child may experience great relief, even sobs and tears, when initially removed from a violent home by a parent who is the victim of domestic violence. But that necessary first step is only the beginning. Most children need immediate counseling—not family therapy but their own counselor so that they can express their loss of respect, even disgust, for the parent who is the victim as well as their fear and anger towards the perpetrator. It is complicated but necessary. Sadly, children who do not receive counseling often end up using threats, intimidation and even violence themselves towards a parent because they have seen it work to get what they want. An impish eight-year-old boy in juvenile court may explain to the judge that the reason he slaps his mother is that he saw her boyfriends do it to get what they wanted. It worked! He imitated them and his mother again was the victim.

The Lake Forest, Washington, Police Department and The Leadership Council teamed up to author a very helpful two-page document, "The Effects of Domestic Violence on Children." (http://www.leadershipcouncil.org) They list four common factors which govern a child's response to domestic violence in the home:

- The child's interpretation of the experience (age influenced);
- How the child has learned to survive and cope with stress;
- The availability of a support network for the child, and
- The ability of the child to accept support and assistance from adults

The fear, sleep disturbances, nightmares and lack of cooperation with others that children from birth to age six experience translate into irritability, hyperactivity, low performance in school, beginning stages of violent and verbally abusive action and difficulty in making friends in elementary and middle school children. For teenagers, exposure to domestic violence can lead to depression, high levels of aggression, delinquent or criminal behavior, teen pregnancy and drug use and loss of respect for the parent-victim.

Those behaviors do not disappear when the violence ends. Skilled therapy for the child is just as important as therapy for the victim who has left the abusive relationship. Good therapy can guide the post-divorce relationship for both the child and victim-parent.

Some of the problems that an abusive parent may exhibit which arise after the separation are:

- A "my way or the highway" attitude towards timesharing, especially the schedule, and a punitive refusal to be at all flexible;
- Disrespect or even contempt for the co-parent expressed verbally in public, especially when children or other adults are present;
- "Forgetting" to return or exchange the child's clothes, electronics or even homework so that the other parent has to drive over to get them, risking a confrontation;
- Belittling the co-parent to the child by being overly indulgent with gifts, inappropriate movies or lax discipline/very late bedtimes;
- Withholding court-ordered child support until demands are met.

A co-parent who is experiencing great relief at being out of the violent household may not recognize these behaviors for what they are: a substitute for power and control. A good therapist can provide practical, age-specific suggestions to deal with the problem without affecting the child's relationship with either parent. After that step, parent coordination and/or mediation may work as therapy has empowered the victim-parent.

An abusive spouse or partner *can* be a good parent to a child once the abusive relationship ends. But it may take good therapy to get to that place.

Stephanie's story is representative of the ten million children and adolescents who witness violence between their parents or caregivers each year. This kind of violence—domestic violence or intimate partner violence—is defined as "a pattern of abusive behavior in any relationship that is used by one partner to gain or maintain power and control over another intimate partner" (US Department of Justice, 2019). Domestic violence occurs in all kinds of families across the socio-economic groups. It can be verbal, physical, sexual, or psychological and it **always** effects the children in the home, regardless of how a parent may think that they are protecting their child from what is happening. A child does not have to see domestic violence to be profoundly affected by the conflict in the family.

Children like Stephanie may develop a variety of problematic emotional and behavioral problems. It's obvious that Stephanie's parents had a terrible coparenting relationship. She had probably witnessed violent acts before, once again caught in the middle. As an only child, she had no allies. The problems are not always easy to recognize but they have long lasting negative consequences for children's physical and mental health and well-being. Child symptoms can include an array of physical, behaviors, social and emotional concerns including anxiety; increased fear; depression; loss of interest in play, school, or friends; sleep problems; night terrors or nightmares; bedwetting; anger; tantrums; and aggression. In adolescents, symptoms continue to become more and more pronounced. These symptoms may include drug use and abuse; alcohol abuse; truancy; oppositional behaviors; aggressive behaviors/fighting; failing grades and school difficulties; depression; social withdrawal and unmanageable anxiety.

For children like Stephanie, life is a constant roller coaster. Children in volatile households strive for both physical and emotional safety but never quite gets their needs met. Helping children feel safe requires an acknowledgment of the negative impacts of exposure to violence and attention to the developmental and emotional needs of the child. Children and adolescents exposed to domestic violence need to be evaluated and treated by mental health professionals. Children can participate in treatment in a variety of ways including individual, group, or family therapy. It is critical for children to regain their sense of safety and trust for the adults who are tasked with protecting them.

If domestic violence is happening in your home, ensure that you are your children find safety. The National Domestic Violence Hotline for victims is 1.800.799.SAFE (7233), 1.800.787.3224 (TTY), or www.thehotline.org. Another popular resource for women is the website www.btr.org, which stands for Betrayal, Trauma, Recovery. In it, former victims of domestic violence nationwide have become trained counselors and provide sessions over Zoom.

Chapter 9
His, Hers and Theirs Times Two

How Folded, Blended and Whipped Families Communicate

Irene: Jack and Rose Marie got married fourteen years ago and had three children: a boy thirteen and identical twin girls age eight. Although both Jack and Rose Marie worked hard at their jobs at a computer tech company and spent all extra time with their children, their marriage suffered and they went through an amicable divorce resulting in an agreement to share the children equally. Their son, Lucas, would soon enter high school, hoping to make the soccer team. The girls, Tracy and Tina, still in elementary school, were just beginning gymnastics, which both parents supported. Jack and Rose Marie pledged to each other that they could make the coparenting in a divorce work, just as they had made their marriage work for years.

A month after the divorce was final, Jack moved in with Susan, who was raising two boys alone as a single mom as their father, David, had walked out on them years ago and the state was still chasing him for child support. The two boys, Cole and Carter, ages ten and seven, loved Jack and bonded with him as a father figure. They also got along well with Lucas, like an older brother, and the twin girls and enjoyed their time with them.

Meanwhile, Rose Marie met a nice man, Eddie, who worked for a computer support company and he and Rose Marie were married after a quick courtship. Eddie had a daughter, Alexia, age sixteen, with his long-time girlfriend, Tammy. Alexia rotated between them amicably. Alexia tolerated Lucas, like she would a younger brother, but she really liked the twins, Tracy and Tina. Alexia's mother, Tammy, couldn't stand Eddie and didn't want to speak to him. They communicated solely by text messages. Tammy liked the fact that Alexia was with other children, but she didn't want anything to interfere with Alexia's dance lessons, as Alexia was a talented tap/jazz dancer who hoped to obtain a scholarship. Tammy's boyfriend, Ryan, ran a local bar/restaurant and was largely out of Alexia's life, although Alexia occasionally visited his bar and he slipped her and her underage friends a few beers.

Surprise! Jack and Susan got pregnant! A new baby girl was delivered the same month that David, the father of Cole and Carter, Susan's two boys, appeared on the scene with a check for back child support and a desire to see his boys again. A permanent domestic violence injunction kept Susan and David from communicating. Everyone was happy about the new baby. Who wouldn't be? But the issue was time sharing. Are you confused by this scenario? So are we, but it is real!

How do we "honor every other weekend" commitments? How should the parents of these many children and stepchildren communicate? How do they coordinate schedules? By text? In one of my cases, they tried that. The result was massive confusion, as whoever sent a text message first about a new activity or change in the schedule acted dominant, often didn't wait for a reply or to see if the co-parent's new relationship and/or stepchildren meshed with the first text, and so on and so on…Instead, as blended families or even folded families, they felt whipped!

While all co-parents need to talk, preferably in person or by phone or email, using text messages for short notifications only, such as "running 15 min late," these entangled co-parents need to call a family council to adjust and coordinate schedules and avoid conflicts. Just remembering all the different last names is a challenge. Amazingly, kids often thrive in these complicated situations because it is never boring, and they are making new friends as long as adults communicate without rancour, hateful words or accusations. Keeping the peace in this tribal situation is essential. No family law judge wants to sort out the complicated situation.

Lisa: How does a text battle begin? Even with the best of intentions, parents often miscommunicate with each other. It is difficult to get the meaning behind the words when communicating via text and the more complex the information, the more difficult it is to effectively communicate it. Children and their lives are complex and need to be treated with the utmost care. One small miscommunication between co-parents can lead to a spiral of misunderstandings, insult and anger that never gets fully resolved and multiplies in blended families with many schedules to observe.

The beginning of a seemingly simple text exchange can end up escalating…

Mom: I want to change the visit on Saturday to 12:30

Dad: I can't do that

Mom: Joey needs to go to a birthday party in the morning

Dad: I can take him

Mom: No, this is a friend of mine

Dad: I said, I can take him

Mom: No, I don't want you to take him

Dad: Then he can't go

Mom: That's not fair to him

Dad: I said, I can take him

Mom: No, I can't have you going to my friend's house

Dad: Then I will pick up Joey at 10:00 as usual

Mom: Joey really wants to go to this party

Dad: I said, I can take him

Mom: You're not being fair

Dad: This is my time with Joey, who's not being fair?

Mom: Fine, then be a jerk, you tell him he can't go to the party

Dad: I will tell him that I offered to take him and you didn't want me to. That's the truth.

And so on until this battle grows out of control and damages not only the ongoing coparenting relationship but also the child's sense of connection to parents, family and stability. Putting the child in the middle of conflict is never healthy and never the only answer to coparenting disagreements. If we approach coparenting with a child-centered view, we can ease the negative impact that conflict has on children. If we are always thinking about what is best for our child, what does our child need, what does our child want and how can we both support our child, we will move towards a more empathetic and supportive solution that allows our child to grow and thrive.

It's true that it is more difficult with the example above of multi-blended families but the goals for all the adults should be the same: child-centered best interest, flexibility and good communication…and a very large scheduling calendar for all!

Chapter 10
The Over Booked Child

Irene: Casey and Jeff were young professionals on track for success: Casey in banking and Jeff as a new partner in a well-known law firm. Their jobs required them to be involved in community activities and what little time they had to spare was devoted to their two sons, Brett, age 9, and Charlie, age 7. Casey and Jeff wanted the boys to be as involved with sports and other extra-curricular activities as they both had been raised. Therefore, after school both boys played soccer on different teams, Brett sang in a youth chorus at their church and Charlie was a Boy Scout.

Casey and Jeff juggled their busy schedules very well, trading off taking a child to a sport or stay home to fix dinner or do homework. Their plates were 100% full and they congratulated themselves on their efficiency—right up until Casey fell in love with the president of her bank. Separation and divorce proceedings followed, and the couple quickly arrived at a 50/50 timesharing schedule, week on/week off, as each considered the other to be a good parent.

Lisa: These days there are so many great opportunities for children that offer a variety of ways to provide entertainment for kids, teach them valuable lessons, give them a base of skill, provide exercise and socialization and help them feel connected to others, both peers and adults within their communities.

That's amazing for our children but we often overload children's schedules and end up creating more challenges for our kids than meant to. By their very nature, children want to do everything. Experience it all, say "yes" and participate in everything. Children are curious, energetic and love to have fun. What children aren't very adept at yet, is creating boundaries and knowing what their limits are and when they need to stop. The over-booking of children has become a monumental problem in our society. Parents are so eager to give their children experiences and keep them busy that they often don't slow down enough to learn what their children are saying, what they are interested in, what they want to pursue, and what they have talent or skill in. Having too much to do is as stressful as having nothing to do. Children do need stimulation and opportunities to explore and experience a variety of extra-curricular activities, however, the stress that many parents create by over-booking their children does much more harm than good.

Children need time to unwind, relax, be calm, hang out with friends, play and rest. Schools are pushing students to do more work at home, so outside of school kids have less time to be kids. The creative process of finding something to do that entertains you is important to development and it is quickly becoming a skill that children lack. Giving children room to grow and stretch on their own is a gift that we can give our children. It's important for parents to decide when enough activity is enough and allow your children to make choices about what one or two things they want to participate in. Extracurricular decision making is an excellent time for parent-child discussion, compromise, and decision making. This is a family time activity that co-parents and children can be involved in. It's especially important in the situation of a separation or divorce. Children are already "bouncing around" between co-parent homes. They may need more time to unwind, relax and discover their inner selves.

Part II
The Toolbox

Chapter 11
Resources Used by Judges

Family law judges often use the term "toolbox" to describe the resources designed to reduce conflict between parents while focusing on the best interest of the children. Experienced family law attorneys often recommend the use of these resources before going to court. Even when they don't the judge can order them and allocate payment between the parties. When used successfully, these resources can substantially reduce family law litigation, its financial and emotional costs. Co-parents cooperate much more effectively if they haven't been attacked, maligned and even shamed in court, not to mention the legal expenses they incur.

As a former family law judge and now a guardian ad litem in family law cases, I've seen first-hand the reaction of parents when these resources are proposed. Some are relieved, as they have wanted family therapy or mediation for a long time. Others are skeptical, sometimes scornful, feeling that the problems are entirely the other parent's fault, and nothing will change. A third group is simply impatient, wanting the divorce to be over and looking to the judge to decide.

I've listened often to Florida Judge Jack Helinger's persuasive speech to divorcing parents:

"I love my job. I'm not afraid to make decisions. It's what I get paid for and I try hard to be good at it. But I've never met your beautiful children. I have no idea what they are like, how they do in school, what sports or recreation or vacations they enjoy. What friends and relatives they have. When they are vulnerable, frail or joyful. As parents, you two know that very well. I don't.

"Yet you are asking me to make decisions that will affect your children for years, maybe for a lifetime. And I'm just a well-paid public servant. A stranger to your family.

"Fortunately, we have valuable resources in our community that can help you two get through this and make decisions in the best interest of your children. Not every community has them. They are far superior to endless litigation in family court.

"I urge you to use these resources. If they don't help, well, I'll be here to make decisions for you. But I bet you will benefit greatly from these resources."

Judge Helinger would always end this speech with a broad encouraging smile.

In the following chapters, let's examine the resources in a family law judge's toolbox. Among them are an understanding of infant and early childhood development, mediation, parent coordination, family therapy, coparenting therapy and the appointment of a guardian ad litem.

Chapter 12
The Beginning: Infant Development

Family law judges who have been educated in Adverse childhood experiences and child development use these "tools" in their toolbox to educate parents—especially young parents—in their infant child's developing brain and the need for good coparenting at this time.

Where do we start...*first comes love, then comes marriage, then comes baby in the baby carriage*—wait—let's rewind that just a bit and go back in time nine months... the sperm meets the egg and forms a zygote which begins to divide and divide again. Through the course of the next 274 days cells divide, multiply, branch out, form primitive neural pathways, and develop into a viable fetus... *then comes baby in the baby carriage.*

Mom and Dad are counting fingers and toes while simple neuronal connections and skills begin to form and will rapidly be followed by more complex circuits and behaviors. With 700 to 1,000 new neuronal connections forming every second parents are the key to helping baby develop early brain pathways. In the meantime, baby begins to absorb the world around her and starts to develop responses that both meet her needs and enable her to develop connections with her caregivers. This developmental process is the serve and return interaction between the baby and her caregiving adults that supports the brain architecture that leads to healthy learning and behavior. As baby's brain develops, it become more and more efficient at lightning-fast communication between neurons that facilitate baby's development of multiple kinds of specialized brain functions... baby is actively smiling, cooing, laughing, flirting and through all of her senses is interacting with the world around her.

Infant's earliest experiences, the relationship between brain function and behavior, help babies learn the important skills of calming, paying attention and developing interest in the world. This learning begins with the most basic form of understanding of cause and effect and leads baby into a complex world of reciprocal interactions and manipulations of the environment to meet her needs.

The developing brain requires the interaction of genes and experience, how your baby was born and what experiences your baby has when they emerge out into the world. We want to think about this development because brain development precedes the appearance of newly acquired behaviors and increasingly complex behavior. The brain will continue to change and adapt to be responsive to the experiences of the interchange between your baby and her environment. During the infant's first 18 months we see brain spurts where brain areas are peaking and guiding baby's early interactions and skill development.

It is during these first months that infants begin to develop the ability to regulate their emotions, focus their attention and explore their environments. As we begin to understand our infant's emerging emotional expression and unique individual style and personality, we learn how to communicate with and meet the needs of our baby. Both infant and caregiver are learning about each other and developing their own special way of getting in synch with each other. During this time, Mommy and baby, and Daddy and baby, begin falling in love. As baby grows, social interactions and new emotional expressions support the development of the parent-child relationship and further support the emerging process of attachment that begins with falling in love.

During these early months of life, every positive, attentive, and calm interaction, increases the baby's ability to self-regulate, calm themselves and connect with the world around them. Babies will learn the concept of turn taking, coordinating behavior with others and the basic foundations for human interaction that support their continuing emotional and behavioral development. Babies become increasing more responsive, sleep for longer periods of time, and eagerly smiling, coo and flirt with their caregiver. During infancy and early childhood, the brain changes with experience. Babies' brains are built in large part through the experiences they have, particularly the social experiences they receive from interacting with their caregivers and their environments.

From birth, babies are capable of affecting the social environment around them. The co-parents in their lives respond differently to the variety of newborn behaviors and signals that their infants create. Babies learn that their caregivers will respond to their signals of distress and be available or unavailable to meet their needs. Caregiver presence is connected to the infant's state of alertness and the relief of distress which further supports the development of the infant-caregiver relationship and early attachment behaviors.

There are countless benefits of early attachment to the development of the baby's brain and body. The earliest expression of effective strategies for coping with the novelty and stress that is part of all human interaction is infant mental health and stands as the basis for future well-being and mental wellness. This system is laying the foundation for the development of self-regulation for baby. This skill is essential for optimal development throughout the course of the lifespan.

The most critical concept in this chapter is that the connection between early social experiences and environmental interactions, including important social experience and relationships, set the babies developmental course. This vital information assists us in helping co-parents and caregivers understand the importance of positive, nurturing, supportive, and reciprocal interactions with their babies. We know that young children's brain development and well-being depends on sensitive responses to babies' bids for attention, interaction and love.

Family law judges trained in infant and early child development will pass on a shorthand version of their training to parents of these children or refer them to child study centers and classes for education. No longer are infants ignored when exposed to high conflict between parents.

Co-parents working in child-centered, collaborative and cooperative ways to support positive relationships between and among caregivers establish the foundation for the healthy brain development that all of our babies deserve to have.

Chapter 13
Mediation

Mediation is a process whereby a neutral third person—usually a lawyer trained in dispute resolution—helps the co-parents reach an agreement as to all or some of the issues in their separation or divorce, including issues involving their children. Many judges require mediation before setting contentious hearings. Many judges order it more than once as difficult issues are brought to court or the case gets close to a final hearing.

Judges have very good reasons for preferring mediation on disputed child issues. "You know your children, I don't," we've heard many judges say. "You two parents love these children and you are the best people to decide their futures, including how much time they spend with each of you, where they will live and what schools they will attend. It's true, you don't agree now but if you both keep an open mind, act in the best interest of your children and participate in good faith in the mediation process, including compromising when called for, you can get this done between the two of you, without my help."

Mediations are set for a full or half day, depending on complexity and the degree of conflict. Parents attend with their attorneys, if they are represented, or on their own if not. Mediators may request brief summaries in writing from each side before the day of the mediation. Once the process begins, the mediator is in charge. The mediator explains the process to each side, defines confidentiality and encourages compromise. Then the mediator separates the parents into different rooms, with their attorneys, and the mediator travels back and forth between them, trying to hammer out an agreement. If a complete or partial settlement is reached, the mediator drafts the agreement, the parents and their attorneys sign it. If the mediation impasses, without an agreement, the parties are back in court. Or for a second or third try at mediation. The judge never knows what was discussed at mediation.

Judges often can provide free or cost-adjusted mediation for low-income families. However, for parents who pay or split the full cost of a skilled mediator, perhaps $200 per hour, it is almost always much less expensive than a court trial or a series of contested hearings.

In family law, financial issues such as alimony, equitable distribution, a spouse's ability to be employed or attorney's fees can dominate the disputes. Children's issues are often held hostage to a full settlement on financial issues. A good mediator detects this strategy and encourages the parents to resolve children's issues for the benefit of the children. A good mediator diffuses the blaming, the shaming, and the anxiety present when parents argue about their children. If those issues are settled, financial disputes become easier to resolve.

Joan Walker is a very experienced, well-regarded family law attorney in St. Petersburg, Florida. She approaches mediation with the same degree of preparation and professionalism she shows in court. She believes in the mediation process, regardless of whether it is court-ordered or voluntary. She knows that children are better served when their parents agree on their issues.

Joan shared with us some tips for a successful mediation:

1. The mediator should be skilled and experienced in mediating family law matters and should have a professional background that provides understanding of the issues and emotions of the parties. While a mediator who is skilled in assisting to resolve commercial cases may have an intellectual understanding of the case, the family law mediator must have an understanding of the emotional components of the case. This is particularly true when children are involved.
2. The mediator should explain at the outset that he or she may spend more time with one party than the other and explain that this is not a sign of partiality, but simply a necessity as some individuals require more time to provide information or ask questions than others do.
3. The mediator should behave in a way towards both sides that is friendly but professional and should never appear to prefer one side over the other. If a party hears laughter coming from the other party's mediation room or sees the mediator in what appears to be a social and private conversation with the other party's attorney, it may appear that there is partiality. It is very difficult to settle a case where one side believes that the deck is stacked against them.

4. The mediator should, at the beginning of the mediation, explain to both parties that they have the right to require the mediator to hold statements of the parties in confidence, if requested. The mediator should explain to both parties the reasons for that confidentiality, and always ask a party if certain information may be shared with the other side before doing so.
5. The mediator should appear to be respectful of each parent's position no matter how difficult that may be. The mediator should attempt to move a party away from an illogical position gradually and by questioning the party about the position in such a way that the party begins to see the lack of reasonableness.
6. If an agreement is reached, in whole or part, the mediator should reduce it to a written agreement, signed by the parties and their attorneys before anyone leaves the mediation. Waiting to commit the agreement to writing for days, or even hours, can cause much difficulty. One party may remember the agreement differently than the other. One party, upon receiving input from friends or relatives, may change his or her mind.

The best argument for mediation in family law is that the parties get to resolve their own disputes. Their agreement is much more easily fulfilled than a Final Judgment rendered after a bitterly litigated final hearing by a judge who truly doesn't know the family.

Makes sense, doesn't it? And the bonus is that a successful mediation can improve communication between parents, helping them avoid future conflicts. Mediation teaches them to listen, to re-consider positions they take that are unreasonable and to value each other as co-parents. Successful mediation makes life much easier for the children.

Chapter 14
Parent Coordination

As a guardian ad litem, I often refer parents to a Parent Coordinator after I'm assigned to the case. Although I'm appointed to be the "voice of the child" and also to look after the child's "best interest," this is a limited appointment. My two roles—voice of the child and the child's best interest—are like bookends. In between the bookends are a whole lot of problems that must be dealt with in a high conflict family law case. The overarching problem is poor communication. That's where Parent Coordination can be of tremendous help.

Communication problems don't begin with the separation or divorce. Poor communication is often the very reason for the divorce. Words exchanged between parents are ignored, misfired, hurtful or destructive. Even the absence of words is a communications failure.

I've sat in court in many contested family law cases that began with poor communication and then escalated into anger, blame, and nearly hatred which grew in proportion to the anxiety and mounting financial costs of the litigation. Unlike the parties in other litigation, co-parents can't walk away and never see each other again. They are linked for a lifetime through their children.

A skilled Parent Coordinator (PC) can help the parents come to a full parenting plan or at least some partial agreements that resolve much of the conflict and hopefully eliminate the need for a contested final hearing on all or many of the disputed issues. More importantly, the skilled PC quickly understands the family dynamics and can develop ways for the parents to communicate post-divorce throughout the child's life. This is a *real* benefit that lasts. That's what I like the most about Parent Coordination: Coaching parents to talk to each other to resolve problems!

The best parent coordinators are skilled mental health professionals who understand the rules governing them, their restrictions and the importance of their role. Generally, the parents pay for this valuable assistance, as it is rarely covered by insurance. That is good for the parents who can afford it, as they demand results. For the parents who can't afford it, I believe that, like mediation, parent coordination should be offered by the court system on a sliding income scale basis. It would be cost-efficient for the entire court system, saving judicial time for the issues that absolutely cannot be resolved. Those are generally financial issues, not issues involving the child.

I view Parent Coordination as a cross between therapy and mediation. Like other types of therapy, parent coordination takes place over several sessions of an hour or more with a skilled therapist. Like mediation, nothing is final until the parents agree. In most states *everything* the parents say during the process is confidential, including their agreements. Unless both parents decide to open their discussions to other professionals, or share with the Court, the agreement they've reached and the process are completely confidential. Confidentiality is extremely important because in the PC process the parents can explode, vent, agree, disagree, express frustration as well as thanks to each other, without the judge or attorneys knowing what happened. Isn't that what we are aiming for? Parents talking to each other, in person, about their child. With the guidance of the PC, parents learn their post-divorce roles and can explore options, alternatives, opinions, and possibilities in the best interest of the child without worrying about what the other parent might say in court.

Different states have laws and family law rules defining and regulating PC counseling. Ethical rules which govern psychologists or other mental health professionals acting as Parent Coordinators also apply. Finally, the court's Order appointing a Parent Coordinator should be carefully reviewed, as it may restrict or expand the PC's role. I've been involved in cases where the Parent Coordinator's role is limited by the terms of the order and the law. I've also been appointed in those cases where Parent Coordinator can make recommendations to the Judge. I see the benefits of each for good post-divorce communication.

Mitchell Kroungold, Ph.D., licensed in forensic psychology and specializing in child and adult psychology, is a superb Parent Coordinator in the Tampa Bay area. I've worked with him often and admire his intellect, compassion, determination, patience and commitment. He helps parents understand and transition into co-parents, resolving conflicts themselves and building a foundation for good coparenting in the future.

Dr Kroungold makes himself accessible and available and has good advice: "Many Parent Coordination issues can be resolved quickly, and quick intervention can prevent the situation from escalating. It is important to ensure that the Parent Coordinator's written communication with the parents is consistent with the order appointing the Parent Coordinator.

"Sometimes simple recommendations can have a significant impact," he said, mentioning a case involving a family who frequently had "horrendous exchanges of the children." He said, "Addressing the exchange can be extremely important as this may be one of the few times when both parents are at the same place with the children. When there is high conflict, children can become the lightning rods for the parental conflict. In a case I handled, the children were old enough that I could recommend that one parent remain in the car, and the other parent remain in the house. The children would transfer their belongings. Once this was implemented, there was a significant decrease in conflict." This is known as curb side pickup or drop-off.

Dr Kroungold said a Parent Coordinator "Can assist the parents to avoid position statements such as holding out for 50/50 timesharing. The collaborative law process strongly advocates for this approach, and it can be extremely helpful when assisting parents to develop a Parenting Plan. It is beneficial to help the parents identify goals that they have for their children. For example, frequent and healthy contact with both parents, minimizing stress related to the divorce, etc. Once there is agreement regarding the goals, it is easier to move past positions and demonstrate to parents that there are many timesharing schedules that would be consistent with the goals agreed to by the parents."

Cases involving domestic violence are more difficult but can be resolved in Parent Coordination, he said. "In one case I assisted the parents to develop a Comprehensive Parenting Plan despite allegations of serious domestic violence. The process was largely conducted by having both parents on the phone during our sessions. I do everything possible to ensure the safety of all participants. In addition to using phone consults instead of in person meetings, I get actively involved and send parents to separate rooms if things get too heated or disrespectful. The goal would be to attempt to bring the parents together for an interview, though this should only happen when the parents feel safe to do so."

Likewise, cases involving children with special needs are difficult but can be resolved with effective Parent Coordination. "It is important to educate parents as well as other professionals involved with the family about special needs that have been identified regarding the children," Dr Kroungold said. "The parents of children with special needs are more likely to get divorced. Parents of children with special needs frequently have very strong opinions about how to meet their children's needs. Thus, there appears to be a disproportionate percentage of families with special needs children in litigation.

"It may be helpful to point out that children's behavior could be a reflection of their special needs rather than alienation. For example, children on the Autistic Spectrum have difficulty with transitions and change. Thus, part of a child's resistance to timesharing may be a manifestation of special needs rather than alienation. I have found it helpful to encourage parents of special needs children to educate themselves, attend support groups and to talk with their child's professional providers," he concluded.

Dr Kroungold found it helpful as a Parent Coordinator to work with other professionals involved in the case, such as the guardian ad litem or the parents mental health therapists. "It typically is very helpful for the professionals to have close and frequent communication, as long as the court order and/or written releases by the parents authorize this communication. Although professionals can sometimes have different points of view, it is most helpful if the professionals can get on the same page or, at least, within the same chapter.

"I recall a case where the guardian ad litem and I agreed that a child who had been resisting timesharing with a parent for a significant period of time would be helped by spending the summer away from both parents, in summer camp. We both testified that this would be in the child's best interest and the judge ordered the child to summer camp. This turned out to be a significant turning point in the case. The mother was motivated to encourage timesharing and the child ended up developing a very positive and healthy relationship with the other parent."

I've been a guardian ad litem in cases that began with open hostility from parents who refused to talk to each other and communicated only by text. After a few sessions with a Parent Coordinator, these same parents were exchanging lengthy e mails and talking over the phone and even in person about school schedules, band and soccer practice, birthday parties and splitting the cost of a new violin. The Parent Coordinator gave them the comfort and tools needed to co-parent effectively and the child benefitted tremendously.

I'm grateful that we have such as skilled professional as Dr Kroungold and other Parent Coordinators in our community.

Chapter 15
Family Therapy

Family therapy is just that, therapy for the family. Family therapy involves multiple members of the family and concentrates on the relationships within the family. It is helpful in increasing communication, resolving problems and working towards smoother, less conflictual interactions. With the emphasis on family relationships, Family therapy can help families achieve better psychological health and well-being. This is an approach that focuses on family problems, which are seen in relation to family interactions, instead of based only on individual members of the family. Family therapists focus on the interactions between family members and how those interactions can help support healthy communication and interactions. Family therapy is frequently short-term and may be used in addition to other types of treatment.

Family therapy can be useful for a variety of family issues. It is particularly useful during times of family change or conflict and in separations, divorce and coparenting. Family therapy may actually prevent a divorce. Issues of adult mental health, couple conflict and coparenting can be discussed and problem solved during family sessions that support better communication and understanding. Family issues such as step-family living, family blending and custody and visitation issues can be discussed and resolved within the family therapy process.

Families often bring an array of challenges to family therapy. In addition to relationship challenges within the family system, families can discuss social stressors, health challenges, child and adolescent behavior, the emotional roller coaster of going through separation, divorce and custody. There are so many feelings when a family is changing. Dealing with the anxiety, depression, grief and loss of our ideal version of our families is always a challenge for us, as adults, and for our children. Investing time in family therapy will promote healthier and happier outcomes for our children and ourselves.

There are many types of family therapy. Several frequently used types include: supportive family therapy, cognitive-behavioral therapy, psychodynamic ideas, systemic family therapy and coparenting therapy.

Supportive Family Therapy is often used to help family members express their feelings regarding a problem that is affecting the entire family. This type of family therapy provides a safe and open environment in which everyone can express what they feel. This is an opportunity for families to get together, and openly talk about the issues that are challenging them, as well as an opportunity for the therapist to offer support and practical problem-solving techniques.

Cognitive-Behavioral Therapy (CBT) techniques attempt to change the ways people think or behave in order to reduce or get rid of the problem. The therapist may assign each individual family member with homework tasks to complete or may create specific behavioral programs in order to help families better manage complex behavioral obstacles and reduce conflict.

Psychodynamic ideas used in family therapy tend to look more into the individual's own unconscious or subconscious minds. This type of therapy attempts to reduce problems by uncovering the underlying problems as many of our family problems are rooted in our own upbringings and past. This method of therapy ties the past with the future and provides individuals with deeper reasons for current challenges and strife in the hope that family members will be able to deal with and work through their difficulties more successfully.

Systemic Family Therapy emphasizes the entire family's feelings. It strives to identify the problems within a family dynamic, as well as the ideas and attitudes of the entire family to uncover what may be going on with the family as whole. After speaking to the children, the therapist gains an understanding of the areas of concern, and attempts to shift the problems, attitudes, and relationships, to a position that is more beneficial, less damaging, or more productive for the family.

Whatever family therapy you choose for your family, you will find that going through therapy together helps everyone in the family heal and move forward towards a new way of interacting and a new state of well-being. Resolving issues early and setting the tone for healthier interactions and greater well-being for children will set the course for a healthier and happier future.

Chapter 16
Coparenting Therapy

Coparenting ng will look different for everyone. It is as unique as each family is. Some coparenting goes great for all parties and some becomes the most destructive part of a child's life. We don't assert that there is only one way to co-parent. There are many ways to co-parent depending on the family, parents, and the children. We would like to help each parent express his or her own values, ideas, and feelings which are at the core of coparenting relationships and decisions.

Coparenting therapists are a mix of parenting coach, mediator, and couples therapist. They provide a structured environment and guidance to work through establishing a positive coparenting situation that works for a particular family. Setting boundaries and guidelines for how to co-parent in the beginning sets the stage for success.

Coparenting therapist's role is to offer expertise around what children often need and assist co-parents to work together on behalf of their family. They help families focus on the shared goal of what is best for the children and help parents stay child-centered in their communication and interactions.

Coparenting is not just for couples that live apart. Coparenting situations can vary greatly including, grandparents, relatives, friends who choose to have a baby, never married couples, and open adoption are just some of the ways that people co-parent. While conflicts and challenges can arise in any relationship, intentionally coparenting couples can plan for challenges even before they arrive. Employing a family therapist or coparenting counselor can, therefore, be a part of separation and divorce planning from the very beginning.

Every person and family brings all sorts of different ideas, experiences, and assumptions to parenting. We are all parented differently and have had an array of early experiences of being parented by our own parents. Some of those experiences are good and some are not so good. Therapy can help sort out how to create a specific way of parenting that suits our family's needs, backgrounds, and beliefs. Coparenting work can help to create a common language and understanding of what our children need, and how co-parents can work more effectively together.

Coparenting are an essential part of the child's ability to recover from a separation and divorce. Many parents acknowledge that they will have difficulty leading their children through the divorce or separation process. Children have complex emotional systems and need support from their parents and close adults. They need to know that there are adults who can manage their own feelings and can help to support the sadness, anger, frustration and confusion that children often feel when their parents separate and divorce.

When there has been a history of pain and conflict in a relationship, the negativity often spills into coparenting. This can take many forms from talking badly about or demeaning a co-parent, litigating past grief, putting children in the middle of the relationship by asking them about a co-parent's personal life, or other hurtful behavior. Most parents struggle with managing frustrations when relationships end. The conflict that exists can lead to continued hurtful or even harmful behavior, leaving co-parents with complex challenges.

A therapist can help advocate for children's needs and support the best possible success in the relationship between the child and their parents. The family can learn to operate differently and become successful negotiators for their child's best interests.

Coparenting therapy can assist co-parents in making child-centered decisions. Struggles with communication are typical and therapy can provide the space that is needed to sort through communication issues and gain valuable skills in conflict resolution, cooperation and communication. These skills can include setting limits, forming agreements, having fair boundaries, and learning to talk and listen with intention.

Often a moderator is needed to help with processing the complicated emotions that come from relationship break downs. There are usually hurt feelings, resentments and anger from one or both parties. Coparenting therapy can help realign co-parents thinking about setting their own feelings aside and staying focused on what is best for the children.

When parents separate, it leaves children navigating between two homes. These pivotal life transitions are painful and challenging for children. Families must stay centered on the important issues about parents providing support for the child's comfort and success at home, what needs to be communicated between the child and parents to help put a child at ease, how much communication between co-parents is helpful and what is hurtful to the child, how similar should rules and routines be at each home, and when there are challenges, should the schedule be disrupted, and for how long. Figuring out how a family balances adjusting and shifting homes during stressful times is critical to children's development and well-being.

There are other complicated issues that coparenting therapy can help with; deciding when and how to introduce new romantic partners or spouses to children, working together to prevent or identify when putting children in the middle of the coparenting relationship, ensuring that children are not asked questions about other co-parent or that co-parent's relationships, defining stepparent roles, agreeing on accountability around school and home life, agreeing on rules across environments, discussing child care arrangements, and issues around physical and mental health providers.

Think of the myriad issues that arise for co-parents: education, sports and other activities, medical and psychological matters, behavior issues, discipline, curfews and over cell phone use.

Whether the coparenting issues seem large or small, significant or miniscule, it is always best to consult with a professional therapist to ensure that you are working from a preventative stance. What is being prevented? Pain and suffering for your children and a lifetime of confusion, anger, resentment, and grief over painful memories of a painful childhood.

Coparenting therapy helps parents with decision making.

Helping parents make decisions is at the heart of coparenting counseling. Therapists help everyone in the family deal with what's in the way of leading first with concern for the child. They don't just insist on this; they use skills as therapists to understand and address what conflicts make that difficult. Their job isn't to be a third set of opinions in making a decision. They give parents space to listen, as well as set aside their opinions enough to truly be curious about the other parent's position. They also help everyone get better at articulating that position.

Parents split for a reason, and usually struggling to communicate or feel heard is part of that. Sometimes therapists simply need to support both parents to get better at being assertive, being less intimidating, taking in what's being said, or not being a pushover so that they can come to a decision that works for the family.

Quite commonly children show a preference for spending time with one parent versus the other. Of course, this can shift over time, and as kids get older, their preferences may become more insistent and sincere. At times, we have to work to confront at what age or under which circumstances a child's wishes should supersede a custody agreement. How can we allow some autonomy or choice on a child's part, while continuing to reinforce the importance of that child's relationship with both parents?

Another huge concern with intentional splitting is that kids' needs, worries and struggles get lost between the two households. Kids' struggles with learning issues, bullying, or even a health concern can fall between the cracks.

Chapter 17
Guardian Ad Litem

Among the cast of characters in a divorce or paternity case—the parents, their lawyers, the judge, the therapists, the mediator and the parent coordinator—is the guardian ad litem, a specially trained advocate for the child. The guardian ad litem (GAL) acts as "the voice of the child" and also makes recommendations that are in "the child's best interest." Voice of the child and the child's best interest: That's the best way to remember the role of the GAL.

Unlike the mediator and parent coordinator, the GAL is appointed by the judge to testify in court about the child's wishes and best interest. There is nothing confidential about the process within the confines of the case. The GAL has extraordinary power to talk to the child, the child's relatives, teachers, therapists, parent coordinators, pediatricians, psychiatrists, psychologists and counselors to get information about the child. The GAL is prohibited from sharing information about the case with others not connected to the case.

With older children, a primary duty of the GAL is to be the "voice of the child." With infants, toddlers or children too young to understand the issues, a primary duty of the GAL is to conduct an investigation and make recommendations as to timesharing, parental responsibility, school designation, relocation—in other words the issues in the case—that are in the "best interest" of the child.

GALs are appointed by the judge often after an agreement between the attorneys for the parents, followed by an order appointing guardian ad litem signed by the judge. The order should contain a waiver of the hearsay objection, so that the GAL can include in the report and in testimony what others have said. In fact, the GAL is the only one in Court who can testify to what the child said, as family law judges do not like children brought into court in divorce cases, the child's therapist is prevented from testifying due to a privilege of confidentiality, and the parents can't testify to what their child said because it is hearsay. This broad ability to investigate, report and testify is the best reason to have a GAL appointed. Often, at hearings, the judge asks the GAL to testify first.

(The judges also use the GAL in dependency court, for child abuse or neglect cases, particularly with children in foster care, when there is a trial on a termination of parental rights or an adoption. Those guardians are most often wonderful, trained volunteers who spend many hours getting to know a child or a family in order to make recommendations for reunification with a parent, termination of parental rights and/or adoption. This chapter deals with GALs in family court, in divorce and paternity cases. In these cases, unless a lawyer takes a case on a pro bono/no charge arrangement, the GALs are paid by the parents on an hourly rate or flat fee basis.)

Irene: When I get a new GAL case, I first set a meeting with each parent at their lawyer's office or somewhere else for those without a lawyer. I explain my role as GAL, go over the order appointing me and the statute, answer any questions and then ask for a "nutshell" version of the case as it is now—not three years ago. I've found it helps if we are on the same page, so I can focus on relevant and immediate issues. I'm careful to tell the parents that I am not the attorney for the child, advocating for what the child wants, but rather the "voice of the child," repeating what the child wants but also what is in the child's best interest. To explain the difference, I give an example of a teenager who dislikes both parents equally, wants to live in a tree fort in the backyard, have pizza delivered nightly, play loud music and have friends visit. If that teenager told me that, I would put it in my report and testify to it before the judge, as I am the "voice of the child". However, I would also add that the tree fort idea is *not* in the teenager's best interest.

I then arrange to see the child at each parent's home. I watch the family interaction and ask the child to give me a tour of the home. This breaks the ice. I then talk to the child alone in a bedroom, observing toys, books, stuffed animals, electronics and, yes, pets. I have petted or held many a gerbil, hamster, guinea pig, cats and dogs and even had a bearded dragon on my shoulder. I've had parakeets chirp on my finger. I passed on stroking a 20-pound snake named Butterscotch curled around a child's neck. I prefer goldfish!

I never ask the children direct, blunt questions about where they want to live or how much time they want to spend with each parent. We talk about school, friends and relatives, after school activities, sports and vacations. I ask what kind of things they do with each parent. I get a feel for the child on that first visit and return again as necessary. Older children call, text and e mail me. I get information about the child from the collateral contacts such as relatives, teachers, therapists, etc., listed above. I speak to the parents when incidents occur that affect the child. I may do an interim report and make recommendations for family therapy or parent coordination if I detect real coparenting problems.

Finally, I testify in Court about what I've seen and heard during my investigation and what the child said to me. I make recommendations for a final parenting plan, including timesharing, residence, schooling and parental responsibility. Often the family court judges adopt my recommendations; sometimes they do not adopt them, or they do so just partially.

Peggy Clarie Senentz is a very experienced, sought-after GAL from South Pasadena, Fl., just south of St. Petersburg. She also has a very busy adoption practice and comes from a large family herself, so she has a lot of experience with children, including her own. Regarding her work as a GAL, she told me:

"In my experience the GAL can serve as an independent voice for the child and also see things outside of the filter of family history and conflict. In some cases, the child is too young to speak directly to us. Looking at their environments, needs and personality, we as GALS can be a source of information to the Court to help create the best timesharing schedule or develop other recommendations to help the child experience two loving homes where the child can thrive and strive to be the best person they can be.

"The GAL experience is more enriched when we can add in the opinions of an older child who can express their wishes to us. The process of having the child's voice heard in my experience helps the child have a sense that they too are a stakeholder in the reorganization of their family, which of course they are."

I would add that as neither Peggy nor I are therapists—most GALs are not—therefore, having family therapists, psychologists or social workers on board helps tremendously.

Part III
Difficult Cases

Chapter 18
Really Difficult Cases

Coparenting* can become more complicated and difficult in certain situations and with certain people. Instead of making decisions as a nuclear family unit, co-parents make decisions separately, looking out after their own best interest as well as the child's. The new circumstances may be positive, such as a new marriage or job promotion requiring a long-distance move. The new circumstances may be negative, such as an escalation of mental health or substance abuse concerns. Parental alienation and child rejection fall into the category of difficult cases that challenge children, parents, family law judges, therapists and guardians ad litem.

There are no easy answers. It is beyond the scope of this book to cover these problems in depth; however, we recognize that difficult situations and negative circumstances complicate coparenting relationships that may already be strained and difficult. In many cases the negative circumstances themselves led to the separation or divorce, such as domestic violence, substance abuse or mental health concerns. When children are involved, we are asking parents to co-parent with a former spouse or partner who may have been abusive during the relationship. If you have children together, you cannot just walk away.

Even in cases without mental health or substance abuse issues, cases are made more difficult by parents insisting on intractable positions, such as no less than 50/50 overnight time sharing. We see this frequently. One reason is that child support is often calculated on the basis of overnights with the child. Another reason is emotional—a feeling you are less a parent if your timesharing is less than your co-parent. Both reasons make the case more difficult and overlook the fact that a parent can have quality time with a child in many places: at school, sporting events, out for lunch or dinner, meeting at a park, bowling, tennis, miniature golf. It doesn't take another overnight to be a good parent. There are opportunities everywhere.

The professionals we have consulted in the following chapters offer good advice. But every situation is unique. The best advice we can give is to seek professional help from referrals through family law attorneys who know the experts in these areas. Many parents are reluctant to use attorneys because of the expense. It is possible, however, and often very practical, to engage an attorney for a few hours of advice about a specific coparenting problem and a referral to the appropriate therapist.

That is money well spent.

*If you wonder why we use "co-parents" rather than "co-parents" it is because we want to stress unity of purpose and cooperation.

Chapter 19
Mental Health and Substance Use

High conflict coparenting relationships are often the result of a mental health disorder in one or both parents. Frequently, the mental health problem is a personality disorder. Personality disorders are enduring patterns of behavior that differ from the norms in our society. Coparenting in these high conflict cases becomes much more difficult when a parent has mental health problems, diagnosed or not. Only a skilled psychotherapist, parent coordinator or family therapist can navigate through the blaming, paranoia, bullying and hysteria often present when the natural anxiety in a divorce is exacerbated by mental health problems.

Dr Wendy Coughlin is a psychotherapist in Florida who achieves success in these situations through managing the mental health issues concurrently with mediating the conflicts between the parents. Often therapy sessions begin with a lot of initial anger, grief and skepticism. Clients need the freedom to express their distress over the separation and changes in the family structure. In her role as a Parent Coordinator, Dr Coughlin helps parents move beyond grief and anger towards effective problem solving. By focusing on the best interests of the children, parents often succeed in developing a Parenting Plan in a few sessions. In doing so, parents learn how to better co-parent respectfully and effectively by focusing on the best interest of their children.

Many family law judges, attorneys and guardians ad litem have referred the parents in high conflict cases to Dr Coughlin because they don't have degrees in psychology or family therapy. They can often make an educated guess to identify mental health problems which are roadblocks to good coparenting. But all of them need an expert to either validate their theories or tell them they are way off base.

Dr Coughlin described how certain mental health conditions create problems in her work as a parent coordinator. Here is a summary of what she said:

Narcissism: People with Narcissistic Personality Disorder are "always right," even when objective evidence is contrary to their beliefs. They are "always right" and easily angered when opposed. This is sometimes the result of early childhood trauma or neglect; however, sometimes it may result from being the extremely indulged and favorite child who always got his or her way. Research has found evidence that all personality disorders may be mildly or moderately influenced by genetics. Narcissists are particularly difficult to treat in individual counseling; often they reject the need for psychological intervention. If an individual with Narcissistic Personality Disorder agrees to seek individual counseling, there must be a release of information and close collaboration between the individual's therapist and the Parenting Coordinator if either intervention will be effective.

Power and Control: Power and control issues may be seen in any, or all, of the personality disordered individuals; these issues also occur in the absence of a defined mental health disturbance. Like the narcissist, domineering personalities have to have their way. It may be a learned or even accepted dynamic in the couple's relationship which surfaces in a divorce and division of responsibilities. The parent coordinator must set parameters to "trap them" into compliance so that they experience the consequences to their actions that they might not have experienced before the separation. By setting parameters for appropriate coparenting behavior, unilateral decisions are immediately identified and can be confronted. Of course, the goal is for the parents to learn to compromise and establish mutually agreed upon standards. If the co-parents are unable to compromise, the Parent Coordinator may be empowered to make non-substantial decisions for the couple; this is particularly helpful in the beginning of the process.

Bi-Polar Disorder: People suffering from Bi-Polar Disorder have unpredictable mood swings unless they stabilize on medication. If taking medication as properly prescribed, these people can function like a normal person. If not on proper medication, you are not going to get anything consistently done in working with them. Everything is erratic and subject to change.

Borderline Personality Disorders: Parents diagnosed with this illness are also impossible to predict. They are all over the map, agreeing to something one session then reversing themselves the next. The therapist has great difficulty maintaining continuity between sessions. Nothing seems to stick from the last session. They are psychologically unstable and have tremendous difficulty trusting and working with a co-parent or therapist. This disorder is best treated in group therapy; immediate referral to group and/or individual counseling. As with any mental health disturbance, when the individual is working in family therapy or parenting coordination, it is highly recommended that releases are signed to share information between the professions helping the family.

Neurotics: This is an old term that we no longer use but certainly applies to many people and current times. The "neurotics" manifest symptoms of anxiety; they benefit from very clear, black and while guidelines. Because they are always worried and projecting doom and gloom, they may ignore parenting agreements or court orders and may attempt to obtain sole parental responsibility to assure the children are safe. To maximize the probability of coparenting compliance, it is helpful to identify consequences if there is a failure to adhere to parenting plans, etc. Stipulated agreements or court orders which provide more timesharing to the compliant parent when the other parent is noncompliant can help assure the rules will be followed.

Substance Abusers: Individuals suffering from Substance Use Disorders are constantly running around in circles. Often, there is a comorbid mental health disorder. It is hard to pin them down. Depending on the severity of the disorder, these individuals may need intense substance abuse treatment as well as education in parenting before they can effectively co-parent. The Substance Use Disorder must be treated, and preferably be in remission, before working on family issues. Substance abuse treatment requires the skills of a specialist; a certified or licensed substance abuse specialist should also be consulted when a parent has an ongoing or recent Substance Use Disorder.

Coparenting with a former partner who has mental health problems may require continued parenting therapy as well as a great deal of patience and lessons on effective, specific communication. If a parent poses a risk to a child, supervised visits may be appropriate. Otherwise, even a parent with a mental health problem may fully participate in timesharing. The delineating factor as to how much timesharing any parent should have is the ability to follow the Parenting Plan, effectively communicate with the co-parent and protect the best interests of the child.

Chapter 20
He's Your Father

Irene: Sam walked out on Lauren for the third and last time when she was five months pregnant with their son. Lauren had no contact with him, and Sam wasn't present for Casey's birth, his Christening or his first three birthdays. Shortly before Casey turned four, Sam was ordered by authorities to pay child support equal to the amount Lauren was getting in food stamps and subsidized housing. Suddenly, Sam showed up at Lauren's doorstep not only wanting to meet his son but demanding a 50/50 time sharing arrangement. "I damn well better be able to raise the kid who is costing me $800 a month in support," he told Lauren.

Lauren's mother and close friend urged her to "tell the deadbeat to take a hike. He wasn't here for Casey's first four years. He doesn't deserve to be his father." Lauren agreed… somewhat. Part of her wanted Casey to know his father and have some sort of relationship with him. She just didn't know how much or how to go about it. She couldn't afford a lawyer. Casey knew nothing about this.

On the other side, Sam's live-in girlfriend Debbie resented the amount Sam paid in child support and urged Sam to get Casey to live with them at least half the time, "as it will cut down on the support you pay now. We could use that money!"

Armed with the court order designating him as Casey's father, Sam went to Casey's private preschool and demanded to see him as well as to take him home for the evening. The owner of the school called Lauren at work and she arrived at the school within 15 minutes. Lauren and Sam got into a loud argument in the parking lot as other parents were arriving to collect their children. Police arrived on the scene but left after determining it was a "family law matter" once Sam showed the court papers listing him as Casey's father. Sam and Lauren continued arguing in the parking lot when school was dismissed, with Casey crying in Lauren's arms. "Who is he?" Casey asked through his tears. "He's your daddy,"

Lauren told him hastily, eager to get home to her nine-month-old daughter and her boyfriend, Bradley, who lives with them.

Before Lauren could leave the preschool, the owner told her they would have to suspend Casey until the family law matter could be resolved, as the school couldn't tolerate the father's demands and the scene in the parking lot. Lauren burst into tears of her own while wiping Casey's tears.

More and more, guardians ad litem and other therapists have met children like Casey, who are understandably upset and confused when an unknown parent comes into the scene. How should this be handled in Casey's best interest?

This is a traumatic experience for Casey and Lauren. Imagine being a mother with a 4-year-old child that you have parented and raised alone to one day have the child's father, who is a stranger to your sweet 4-year-old, show up and demand equal time. There are so many ways to have prevented this from happening and I hope that reading this will help you think through those ways before disaster strikes. Perhaps a few questions to help you think through those long-lost possibilities. What were the legal options? Could Lauren have reached out early in Casey's life to discover her options for sole custody with no visitation? Could Lauren have considered contacting Sam regarding a joint agreement on how they might parent Casey? Could a coparenting discussion have helped Sam and Lauren think through Casey's future needs together? Could Sam have decided early on whether he wanted to be involved in Casey's life and what that might look like? Could Sam and Lauren have come to an agreement about what financial support and other supports were needed to raise Casey? Could Lauren have introduced the idea of Sam as Casey's father to him when he was able to understand the concept of having two parents? There are so many ways that this might have been prevented or made easier for Casey, Lauren and Sam. But the situation is now a crisis and an emotional trauma that will need to be carefully dealt with.

We may imagine what is happening in the thoughts and feelings of the adults in this scenario: anger, resentment, frustration, fear, panic, or sadness. But putting ourselves into the child's perspective is critical to help support Casey in his understanding of this situation and help him through this difficult time in his development. Young children experience all of the feelings that adults experience. The wide emotional reaction that Lauren is experiencing will also be experienced by Casey. In addition to Casey's own fears of the "stranger", the fighting, the police arriving, the crying and shouting, Casey will also be absorbing all of the negative feelings shown in front of him by his parents and caregivers at school. Children are emotional sponges that soak up all of the feeling that adults express, especially the adults that they have attachment relationships with. Adults are emotional mirrors for children and not only teach their children about feelings and how to manage their feelings but they can also overwhelm young children with big, scary feelings that make children feel fearful, unsafe, and threatened.

What should happen next for Lauren and Sam to be able to help Casey understand this difficult situation? Lauren should take Casey home to a safe space for him and talk with him, calmly reassuring him that things will be OK. Lauren should explain that they will be all right and that the adults will figure this situation out. Lauren should reassure Casey that he is safe and that she will always be there to make sure he is safe. Lauren can then introduce the story of Casey's father and why he is just coming into their lives now. This could be explained in a 4-year-old language by saying that when Casey was born that Lauren and Casey's father did not want to be together anymore because they didn't get along very well. This is most likely the truth and will reassure Casey that it was not his fault that his father left. Lauren could also let Casey know that his father was not ready to be a Dad yet but that now he is older and he feels ready to be a Dad. Children understand readiness and this concept also puts the responsibility for the situation on the adults rather than on the child. Realistic and meaningful conversation about what may happen would also help Casey feel secure that his parents are taking care of this problem and will resolve it in the best way possible for Casey. Perhaps some conversation about the possibility of Casey meeting his father and doing something fun together might lighten the mood and also help to introduce the idea that it is likely that Casey will be spending some kind of time with Sam. This can be discussed in a positive way that will help Casey think about Sam as not threatening but rather as an opportunity for positive adult interaction and connection, which all children need and love.

Hopefully, Sam will be patient and work with Lauren in Casey's best interest. If not, both will need good family law attorneys.

Chapter 21
Relocation

Not many people anticipate that after having a child with another person they will be prohibited from moving with that child to another city, state or country—even for a better job, higher salary or a new marriage—without the other parent's permission or a court order. That is shocking to many parents, but it is an essential part of family law in most states, usually governed by statute.

Relocation statutes vary, even in terms of what constitutes a relocation. In Florida it is a move or intended move by one parent more than 50 miles further away from the other parent. Some states use 100 miles, but not across state lines. Some states use county lines to define relocation, as a move to another county usually means a change in school districts. School changes and timesharing splits are paramount. A parent who has majority timesharing is more likely to win a relocation case than the parent who has 50% timesharing, a current trend in many states. Best interest of the child governs most court decisions. The active participation of both mom and dad in the whole of the child's life is generally considered to be in the child's best interest.

Relocation cases are extremely difficult for the parents, the children, relatives and especially for the judge who must decide the issue. Everything, including a new job, housing, schools, transportation, remains up in the air until a settlement or a court ruling occurs. Settlements are rare because most divorced parents do not want their child moving far away.

Guardians ad litem have had some heart-breaking relocation cases. Particularly those where the parents are getting along fine, the timesharing is working well, both parents are involved in school and the child's activities and coparenting is successful.

Jan and Skip sat together at their 11-year-old twin sons' soccer games, cheering for Robby and Rex and their team. They exchanged information about the twins' school, tutoring and medical issues and gave each other updates during the exchanges. They shared their sons on a 50/50 timesharing arrangement, flexible when necessary. Both had remarried and they got along with the new spouses. Many of their divorced friends envied their relationship. Then Skip got the opportunity to move to Hawaii, doubling his salary through a promotion from his employer, a software development company. Of course, he wanted to take the promotion, and take his twin sons with him and his wife to Hawaii.

Skip promised Jan extra timesharing in the summer and during other school holidays, but Jan was devastated. She was very involved in her twins' schooling and sports. Frankly, she had grown used to the 50/50 timesharing and she liked the free time it provided.

The judge had to weigh and balance the competing factors of substantially more income to Skip to support his family and the loss to Jan of meaningful timesharing; of the opportunity for a big promotion leading to a high level executive position for Skip back at the home office in a few years, versus the mother taking a back seat on school issues as a "vacation only" mom, or cutting the father out of the twins' lives unless he turns down the promotion or spends the entire salary increase on airfare.

You be the judge! Tough decision, isn't it? Hard to find a compromise that is in the best interest of the children.

Another case was even more complicated, with implications for the entire extended, blended family.

Crystal and Mike had daughters ages six and eight when they divorced. Within two years, both had acquired significant others. Crystal's new husband, James, had a fourteen-year-old son he shared equally with his ex-wife, Toni. Mike moved in with Lindsay, a single mom raising a three-year-old daughter. Lindsay soon became pregnant and Mike became a father again—a baby boy who his two girls adored. Timesharing schedules were complicated, but the five adults worked hard to make them compatible. Then Crystal, a sales agent for a high-end condominium development company, got notice that she was being transferred across the state. As the major breadwinner for the family, she couldn't say no. Of course, she wants to take along her new husband, James, her girls and his son.

Now figure this one out. How many lives are impacted by Crystal's move? If Crystal's ex, Mike doesn't agree that their girls can move with her, or James' ex, Toni, won't let their son go, both Crystal and Mike have to petition the family court to relocate those children across the state. In Florida, unlike many states, there is no presumption for or against relocation. Factors the judge has to consider include the relationship between the parents and children, the child's preference, whether the general quality of life will be enhanced, the reasons for opposition to the relocation, preserving the relationship between the parents and children as well as the employment and economic circumstances of each parent.

No one thought when the knot was tied, or they moved in together, and a child was born, that it would get this complicated. But in today's world of transient relationships, it often does.

This is a complexity that is not easily resolved. While we think about the overall well-being of the family in these situations, it is imperative that the children's best interest be front and center of the decision making here.

Let's keep in mind some important child-centered concepts that may help during the decision-making process. Developmentally, children tend to blame themselves for negative things that happen in their families and in their environments. If the adults making the decisions about where children will live and who will care for them cannot agree, this puts an unhealthy emotional burden on the child.

Often children show a preference for spending time with one parent versus the other. This is natural and can change over time. When children grow and mature, their preferences may become more insistent and sincere. At times, we must work to confront at what age or under which circumstances a child's wishes should supersede a custody agreement. How do we allow some autonomy or choice on a child's part, while continuing to reinforce the importance of that child's relationship with both parents?

Moving between homes long distance is always a particular challenge for coparenting and for families in general. Depending on the circumstances and on distance, this can create drastic changes in how coparenting happens and how children live their lives. The hard work for supporting children through the emotional changes in these situations can be intense and long lasting. Thinking about if a child will need to change schools, how they communicate with each parent, stay in touch with their adult and peer support systems, and does this feel like a loss for the child and how can they be supported through the grieving process.

One of the most common reasons families parenting separately seek coparenting counseling is behavioral problems in their children. Behavior has meaning and acting-out behavior is often best seen as a child communicating to their parents that something in the arrangement is not working. If we can help parents get on the same page, manage disagreements and old hurts, and communicate consistently and without conflict, often the behavior problems will diminish or vanish.

With young children, behavior problems are often how stress, emotional strain or a lack of continuity between coparenting households can present. While the cause of behavior problems, especially in young children, is complex, establishing clear expectations and routines, and an agreed-upon system of responding to acting-out behavior is a critical first step to resolving difficult situations and feelings for the child.

Children see and hear everything. They are consistently keen observers of their parents' behavior and conflict. Separation, divorce, or living in two different and varied households can create situations where children's needs, worries, and struggles get lost between the two parents and their two households. Children who aren't supported with steady and cooperative coparenting may feel so much stress that they will struggle with mental health issues, behavioral problems, learning issues, bullying, or physical health concerns that will become long-term challenges for them and their sense of safety, joy and well-being.

Chapter 22
When a Child Resists a Parent

"I just don't like him," nine-year-old girl Carly answered when her guardian ad litem asked why she didn't want to spend time with her father, a responsible person who had lived with her and her mother in their marriage since her birth, without incidents, until the recent separation and divorce, which was agreed upon and fairly amicable. "Now that they are divorced, my mother doesn't have to spend overnights with him. Why should I?"

Wow. A child this direct in a family law case was unusual. Her parents were hard-working professionals: Dad was a lawyer, mom a nurse. According to both they had drifted apart, had different friends and activities, and agreed that divorce was best. They quickly resolved financial issues. The only thing in the way of a final hearing was Carly's stubborn insistence that she did not want to spend *any* overnights with her father. Her resistance stood in the way of an agreed-upon parenting plan. Dad simply wanted every other long weekend, Friday after school until Monday morning, and an overnight during the off week. Mom didn't object. Carly did!

In their book, *Overcoming the Coparenting Trap: Essential Parenting Skills When a Child Resists a Parent,* by John A. Moran, Ph.D., Tyler Sullivan and Matthew Sullivan, Ph.D., the authors confront this problem up front in their introduction:

"Why do children resist a parent? Is it because the parent deserves it? Is it because the favored parent has undermined the child's relationship with the resisted parent, either consciously or unconsciously? Is it because the resisted parent did not establish a secure bond with the child during the marital years? Does the child prefer one parent because of differences in parenting styles, discipline or more material advantages in one home? Are their lifestyle elements that forge the child's alliance with one parent, such as shared religious beliefs, recreational interests or other gender-based preferences.

"Has the parent forged a relationship with an intimate other whom the child resists, or did the new relationship begin in a manner that the child finds morally objectionable? Or has the child been caught in a series of disputes between the co-parents that lead him to side with one parent against the other? Each of these possibilities, and more, need to be considered to understand and describe the factors that lead a child to resist a relationship with a parent. And it may be that different factors contribute to the process in different ways at different points in time. It is complicated."

Indeed, it is complicated! That is the best description of the problem. It is an obscure, delicate and moving target—different reasons at different times for different children. Especially during the stress of litigation, it is too easy to blame parental alienation, misbehavior, disrespect or psychological issues of the child or even outside influences. While understanding the root cause is important, it is more effective to work proactively to repair the relationship between the child and the resisted parent. (An exception, of course, would be actual child abuse or neglect, when contact may need to be limited or supervised.)

Guardians ad litem encounter child resistance more often in adolescent girls who are the only child of their parents or are distanced from a sibling by gender and/or age. Rare, is it seen in sibling groups of three or more children, rarely in teenagers and almost never in boys. I think that is because adolescent girls are so sensitive, going through so many changes, and increasingly aware of relationship problems. Children who navigate time sharing with close siblings are like a flock of ducks: they do things together and have the comfort of each other. Teenagers are so immersed in their own lives that they may ignore adults around them. Boys often can be bought off with electronics or mechanical projects.

But adolescent girls, whew! Often mom becomes the "preferred parent" if she is a stay-at-home mom, the parent in charge of family events, discipline, school activities and daily comfort. This is especially true if dad is rarely at home, distracted by work and uninvolved. I have had a few divorce cases where professional parents have switched traditional roles and dad is the stay-at-home parent, often working from home. Not surprisingly, that adolescent girl bonds to dad and resists time sharing with mom. I rarely see resistance when the nurturing is equal: either both parents totally involved in the child's life or both parents working so hard that a nanny or grandparent raises the child.

Dr Eric L. Rosen a psychologist is the Clearwater area of Florida, specializes in child resistance cases in his therapeutic practice. Dr Rosen looks at reunification therapy as a "complex set of emotional gears operating within fractured family relationships, subsumed frequently under legal mandate and scrutiny, activated among participants compelled to work together under relationship parameters oftentimes not intended by voluntary design." Yes, it sounds complicated, but it may just mean an adolescent girl who hasn't "volunteered" to spend alternate weekends or even a weekday with a parent!

Dr Rosen continued: "At the heart is a dissolution of hearts as parents once joined in love, the pursuit of shared dreams and bonded through raising children, find life changing and at times unravelling, Pain turns into anger, bitterness, apathy and indifference. Battles center around money, possessions, unresolved betrayals and hurt with courts and attorneys embroiled in the fight. What was once private and behind closed doors becomes public, shaming and uncomfortable. And children become collateral damage, if not the treasures of protection or pursuit. Children in the climate of heated divorce may feel insecure or grieving what was once stable; however, many feel relieved that heated feelings or cold indifference has become less noticeable.

"It is important to note that children may not always respond emotionally in the same fashion as adults would in certain situations. It is not uncommon for children to shut down emotionally, act as though nothing is wrong or claim indifference. More importantly, understanding a child's reactions and mental state may require patience and understanding to decode child behavior, and peer through the child veil of indifference to uncover authentic thoughts and feelings.

"For example, if attachment was ill formed prior to a separation or divorce, the child may find the non-favored parent to somehow be unnecessary."

Unnecessary. That's the word that best describes the reason for child resistance. Not hate, not fear, not disgust. *Just unnecessary.* This seems to fly in the face of a long-held belief that children yearn for approval and attention from both parents, even and especially after a separation or divorce. Yet if one parent has met all the child's needs and continues to do so, is the other parent irrelevant?

In their booklet, *Overcoming the* Coparenting *Trap,* authors John Moran, Tyler Sullivan and Matthew Sullivan have listed some skills for the resisted parent that Dr Rosen and other family therapists suggest. Summarizing a few of them:

* Do not make long-winded or highly emotional statements about how much you love and miss your child. Simple statements that you love them should suffice.

* Do not insist on your child hugging or kissing you or your family members.

* Show affection by sending cards and/or gifts for birthdays and holidays, even if they are returned.

* Show affection by showing up at extracurricular school and sporting events (unless prohibited by a court order, or the parents have agreed not to attend activities at the same time.) *Frankly, for good* coparenting *both parents should be able to attend all activities, even together.*

* Show you care by considering your child's wish not to be around someone you are dating.

* Discourage extended family from contacting your child directly if he/she does not want it. Be sure to tell family members not to express their thoughts about the family conflict, who is to blame and how the child should be acting towards you and them.

Patience, a great deal of it, is required of the resisted parent. The longer the child resists, the more difficult it is to repair the relationship; yet patience, biting one's tongue, controlling impulses to lash out---all that is required of the resisted parent.

Dr Rosen and other family therapists suggest activities to renew or even create a parent-child bond, ranging from as simple as board games, making breakfast together or library trips to biking, fishing or hiking. Shopping for expensive items, especially a new cell phone, or going only to movies the child chooses may be manipulative on the child's part. In extreme cases, there are reunification camps around the country for intensive therapy.

In most cases, the child will open up and communication will improve. When this happens, the authors of *Overcoming the Coparenting Trap* have additional parenting tips, which I found useful for many situations with difficult children:

"* Work around highly emotional issues. If asked to talk directly about family relationships, a resisting child will typically shut down or argue, without giving thoughtful consideration to the ideas the parent wants the child to understand.

* Carefully orchestrate talks about sensitive issues. For example, ask the child if it is a good time to talk about a touchy subject and if the child says it is

not, agree to talk later, or maybe ask for another time to schedule the conversation.

* Do not dismiss the child's negative attitudes and emotions by saying they should not be angry or afraid of you. Do not say that their feelings are caused by the preferred parent, or that their thoughts come from the preferred parent. The word "brainwashed" is a flashpoint for conflict. Say something like, "I get that you are really angry and disappointed in me. I want to respect those feelings and still try to make the best of our time together. I don't agree with much of what you are saying, but we probably can't talk through that at this point, so let's focus on making the best of things right now and look forward to a time when we will be able to talk about some of these things and actually achieve a clearer understanding of what happened and what went wrong."

* Avoid arguing about what is true. Arguing about the facts of what happened, or what the facts mean, makes people feel discounted, defensive, self-righteous, resentful and closed to relationship. It may be possible to clarify simple facts about what happened in the past, like whether a vacation trip was in June or July, but the child's memories are clouded by their interpretations that probably are not up for reconsideration.

* Avoid asking why your child is acting a certain way: Children may be incapable of verbalizing their feelings or hesitant because they feel intimidated.

* Children caught in the middle are very aware of the location of their parents and may act differently depending on who is present. A child's loyalty conflict is heightened when both parents are present. Be aware of how the presence of siblings, especially older brothers or sisters, may affect a child's behavior and plan accordingly."

Always, forgiveness is the first step to healing. It is being a good person, a good parent, a good child.

Chapter 23
Who's Behind This?

Button Pushing, Social Media Stalking and Other Coparenting Hijinks

At least when co-parents are speaking to each other, in person or by phone, they know who is talking. That seems elementary, something we took for granted before text messages, e mail and social media became the primary communication for co-parents. Young co-parents, millennials, use electronic media almost exclusively. It has caused some unbelievable problems.

Casey and Michael had been divorced longer than their three-year-old marriage. Because they lived just a few blocks from each other and shared their two young boys week on/week off, they saw each other rather frequently at school events, in the neighborhood and with some mutual friends. Raw emotions had healed since their separation and divorce, and they found a good coparenting relationship as they were focused on the best interest of the boys. They actually enjoyed sharing stories about them with each other. Then Amber, Michael's girlfriend, moved in with him.

Casey liked Amber at first because she was good to the boys. However, soon Michael began to distance himself by cutting their conversations short, saying he preferred to text and e mail. Soon he was opening old wounds, reminding her of "poor discipline" and "spoiling the boys while still living beyond your means, like you used to do." Michael sent her a text message saying he was going to seek a reduction in child support.

Casey was hurt, replying to Michael that this "was all behind us and you are a jerk as usual for bringing it up." Michael responded with some foul language and the next time they saw each other Casey wouldn't speak to him. You guessed it! Michael had delegated to Amber the "chore," as he considered it, of messaging with Casey. After all, it was Amber's idea. However, Michael had no idea of the mischief Amber was causing, all in Michael's name.

In another case, Troy and Michelle married when they each had children from previous relationships, and now a beautiful five-year-old princess from their own union. All the children got along well and they were happy and felt blessed. Then Michelle's ex-husband Sam got a message through social media that Michelle was "cheating on Troy just like she had on you." Sam didn't know the messenger but he felt it to be true as Michelle had cheated on him, not just with Troy but others. So Sam found Troy's Facebook and Twitter Accounts and forwarded the message to Troy, without identifying himself. Troy had a few drinks after reading it, blew up at Michelle and stormed out of the house. Their five-year-old daughter witnessed the scene he caused and sobbed in her mother's arms.

In another case, Regina, a nurse and very busy and important health department employee changed jobs to work for a private physician. Regina and her second husband, Jeb, were in favor of the move because although Regina's salary was less, the benefits were similar and the stress and long hours were gone, allowing Regina to be at home more with the couple's toddler son. Sounds like a winner, right? Until Facebook posts turned up alleging that Regina had a drug problem, was forced out of her government job to take private employment where she could "easily steal her drugs." The Facebook posts eventually reached Reginia's physician boss, who didn't like controversy and terminated her employment. The posts were too numerous and hard to track. Reginia collapsed in shame and was hospitalized for a mental breakdown.

In all these cases, electronic communications were used destructively and intending to harm. In all these cases, the one causing mischief, doing real harm, was a woman—a second wife or new girlfriend. Women are relationship centered. Most times that is good and used positively. But sometimes women who are past or current wives or lovers of the same man start to push each other's buttons in ways never contemplated by their partner. It may be triggered by resentment over child support paid to a former spouse, or timesharing that interferes with the new family's schedule, or just buried anger or jealousy that another woman came before them. The harm can be catastrophic and can impact the children who don't understand the anger expressed between two families.

The solution is easy to express but hard to control. Except for emergencies involving the children, or simple text messages like "running 10 minutes late," all communications should take place between the parents. Only in-person or telephone conversations guarantee this. So, in addition to the many benefits that comes from *real* conversations, it is the only way to guarantee that the person communicating is the one you intended it to be.

Coparenting has its own built-in difficulties. We simply do not need to add electronic hijinks to the mix. Complexity breeds complexity. Bringing a third person from a new relationship into the coparenting relationship often has messy consequences. When co-parents begin new relationships there is often a shift in parenting roles and this can create hurt and anger if not done thoughtfully.

Setting boundaries around who will communicate in the coparenting relationship is top priority. Those initial conversations between new partners about who will communicate and how they will communicate sets the course for the future. Formal family meetings about how communication will occur can establish boundaries and flow of communication that prevent misunderstandings or in the worst-case scenarios, intentionally hurtful communication.

Having mutually agreed upon rules of engagement can be a preventative approach and it can also serve as a proactive way of ensuring that you and your co-parent keep the conflict out of your relationship or minimize conflict that exists. As the models of appropriate and kind behavior for our children, we have the responsibility to ensure that we are proud of our actions and that they are teaching our children the ways that we want them to act in the future. We should expect this from ourselves and from everyone who has an impact on our children. This includes the partners we choose to be with.

Chapter 24
"Battle of the Therapists over Texts"

Robin and Mark were highly educated college professors who considered themselves, and each other, as voices of reason—that is until Mark fell in love with a graduate student and filed for divorce. Robin talked herself out of her personal hurt, but she was heartbroken that their eight-year-old twin sons wouldn't grow up in an "intact" home. She was fearful, very fearful, that they would be caught in the middle of a custody battle, or at least a competition between herself and Mark for the twins' attention and affection. She should know. She was a child of an acrimonious divorce herself. She had been in and out of therapy since her teenage years. She found therapy helpful and recommended it to Mark for himself as they worked through their divorce.

The twins, Teddy and Tyler, slowly adapted to the 50/50 time sharing schedule. They were equally bonded to each parent, which meant they genuinely missed Robin when they were with Mark, and missed Mark when they were with Robin. They told their grandparents that what they wanted for Christmas was "for mom and dad to live together again." Teddy and Tyler were in separate third grade classes; both teachers told the parents they seemed depressed in class and had trouble maintaining attention. Robin suggested therapy for the twins. Mark consulted his own therapist and then reluctantly agreed.

After her first session with the twins, the therapist Robin and Mark agreed upon strongly recommended separate therapists for each twin, as the twins had expressed difficulties with each other during this stressful time. Teddy was outgoing and athletic; Tyler was shy and musical. They disagreed on their activities, as did Robin and Mark. In fact, along with religion as Robin was Catholic and Mark was Jewish, this was an issue they battled over during the divorce.

The parents and their attorneys appeared before the judge for an initial hearing. He ordered that Robin and Mark first engage a parent coordinator, a mental health professional with expertise in helping divorcing parents resolve their disputes, and then attend a mediation before the judge would set the case for final hearing. Counting the attorneys and therapists, there were now seven professionals involved in the case as well as a mediator to be chosen soon. Robin and Mark had good jobs at their universities, but they couldn't afford to take much time off work. They had students to think of, as well as employment security, and now they had to drive Teddy and Tyler to their separate therapists. To avoid further emotional stress, Robin and Mark agreed to communicate only by text, except for their meetings with the parent coordinator. E mail could be used for longer messages. The therapists agreed to use those methods too, outside of their personal sessions with their patient, as they were aware of the parents' busy schedules.

Almost like attorneys, each therapist's duty and loyalty was to that particular patient. Although the texts and e mails between the parents were free of profanity and name calling, there was plenty of guilt tossed around. Each parent shared the other's critical messages with their own therapists and received replies by text or e mails. To Robin and Mark, it began to seem like warfare with their advocates lined up on each side and the twins' therapists legally restricted as to how much they could reveal.

What problems do we see for the twins and their parents in this situation? What is a better suggestion? A family therapist to cut through this? Personal contact in lieu of so many texts?

Lisa: Sometimes so many professionals working with one family really is **too many** professionals. There are sound clinical reasons to use one therapist for all family members, individually and as a family unit. A licensed and experienced therapist can develop one-on-one relationships with each family member and with the family as a unit, without taking sides or aligning with one family member. In a family systems therapy approach, the family is seen as an emotional unit with each family member bringing a separate point of view, separate emotions and ideas. Each member is integral in the way the family system works, the flow of communication, the level of support they can give each other and the resolution of difficult circumstances and conflict. When one therapist works with each family member, there is the opportunity for the therapist to get to know each family member, understand their points of view and emotional processes and then integrate that individual's needs into the work that is done with the entire family. This can be varied, and all relationships should be considered; the relationship between the twins, the relationships between each twin and each of their parents, and the relationship between the parents. In general, the family is guided to resolve conflict, process complicated emotions, and strengthen relationships through the support of one therapist who knows each family member and the family as a whole. This often reduces the stress of having so many professionals see a family.

Building trust between the therapist and the family is an important step in the therapeutic process. Each family member must feel safe to share their experiences and open themselves up to the process. In addition to being necessary for the family to heal and move forward, this building of trust is translated from the therapeutic relationships to the family relationships where trust has often been broken and family members are not feeling trusting of each other or safe to share their thoughts and feelings. The safety of this relationship will eventually become part of the family interactions and sets the stage for more positive coparenting and more joyful experiences for all family members.

When building the relationship between the co-parents, the therapist will work to build a supportive environment between the co-parents. This happens through the development of mutually agreed upon interactions that support good communication, fairness and respect. It is with this effort that co-parents can once again build in the security and safety in their relationship that children need to feel to in order to grow and develop in emotionally healthy ways.

Shared therapy can also help co-parents and their children build deeper understanding of what each child's needs are. Ensuring that each parent is aware of and responsive to the individual needs of each child is critically important for children to develop along an emotionally healthy trajectory. Parents should know what their child's feelings, fears, needs, and wishes are so that the child feels heard and seen in the coparenting process. Often co-parents get so caught up in their own feelings that they forget the real reason that they are at odds. It is because every parent loves their children truly and deeply and they want the best for them. Unfortunately, that is sometimes forgotten in the midst of intense hurt and anger over a relationship break up. It is for this reason that we must be constantly reminding ourselves to stay child-centered. This means always putting the needs of the child first, remembering that we are to nurture and love a child, our children. If co-parents work together, remembering to keep what is best for the children in their minds, they become more empathetic, more connected and better parents.

Chapter 25
Coparenting with A Pseudo Stranger

First, what is a pseudo stranger? Why would you have to co-parent with one? Let's look at what happened to Brian and Sally at the office Christmas party.

Too much alcohol, no spouses present, a good band at a nice hotel and---you guessed it---nine months later Sally brought a healthy baby girl home from the hospital. While she tried to figure out life as a single mom, Brian worked on repairing his marriage as well as his relationship with his son and daughter in college, who both thought that the situation was "disgusting."

Brian realized during Sally's pregnancy that he was going to have to pay her significant child support, due to the disparity in their incomes. He was an important manager in the brokerage firm with a high six-figure income; she a junior assistant at a starting salary. He had no problem with this. What concerned him, though, and it came up in marriage counseling with his wife Marlene, was the extent of involvement he wanted with his baby girl, Ariel. Brian surprised himself by feeling that he wanted to see Ariel frequently and to be a part of her life. Marlene surprised him even more by agreeing with him, as long as he had absolutely no relationship with Sally, who had transferred to a different department in the brokerage firm. Marlene confided that she had experienced "empty nest" feelings since their daughter went away to college. The presence of sweet Ariel in their home might be a blessing.

Sally was the problem. She wasn't happy in her new department in the firm. While she loved Ariel to death and thought the perfect baby girl was the best thing that had happened to her, she didn't want Brian involved in the child's life, except of course for child support. In fact, she wanted to move from the East Coast back to southern California where her mother and sister still lived.

A week after Sally told Brian of her plans to move and the new address for his child support payments, Sally was served at work with a paternity lawsuit containing a request for an injunction prohibiting her from moving Ariel out of the county. She sent Brian a blistering text message filled with shorthand expletives, hired a lawyer and soon found herself on the losing side in court. As everyone agreed that Brian was the father, the judge ruled, Brian was entitled to time sharing rights which would be limited now but increased as Ariel became a toddler. The judge sent the parents to mediation to work out a coparenting agreement and a time-sharing schedule consistent with his ruling.

Before even leaving the courthouse, Brian sent Sally a nasty text message asking how many others Sally "had spread her legs for," accusing her of trying to cut off his rights to Ariel and failing, finally demanding a visit with Ariel at his home. Sally was quick to reply, again using expletives and stating there was only "one thing I wish to cut off!" Sally refused the requested visit and the parties had no other contact before the mediation.

How successful do you think this mediation will be? What should the mediator focus on? What kind of introduction to her birth father might Ariel expect? What can be done to improve the situation?

The concept of mediation to parents who don't agree on anything is a challenge for everyone involved. It is particularly difficult when positive feelings of regard between the two parents never existed. Parents who had been in a romantic relationship at some point will have some positive memories of the attributes of the other person. When the parents are strangers this is unlikely and the negative emotions connected with the argument get wrapped around the negative impressions that they have about each other's characters. This mediation has many barriers to overcome.

The facts are that both Brian and Sally are Ariel's parents. They both have rights and responsibilities in the parenting of Ariel. This will be the focus of the mediation, the acknowledgment that both parents will need to be included in the decision making for and the parenting of Ariel moving forward. Whether they like it or not, this is how it will have to be. The more work that can be done in the beginning with helping both parents come to terms with this and agree that they will work together in the best interest of Ariel is the key to the mediation. The subject of relocation will also be a primary topic of discussion in the beginning but can only be successfully dealt with after both parents have come to terms with the fact that they are now responsible for working out the best possible circumstances for coparenting their baby.

Perhaps the mediator could move the parents towards agreeing that some coparenting counseling could be beneficial for Ariel. After all, for the next 18 years, both parents will need to figure out how to help raise Ariel and how to support Ariel's development without burdening her with animosity towards each other. The best-case scenario is that coparenting supports be used in the beginning of this coparenting relationship. The best possible outcomes will occur if some level of successful communication, coordination and support happen in the coparenting relationship.

Ariel is still a baby and should start to get to know her father now. Time together to begin to bond and start developing the needed connection for a secure attachment relationship is important. Besides getting to know each other, Brian and Ariel need to begin nurturing the parent-child bond that will ensure healthy parenting for years to come. Sally and Brian need to start get used to sharing Ariel, start working on communication and respect for each other, and focus on a child-centered relationship that adds joy to Ariel's life rather than making her life more complicated.

Chapter 26
Children with Different Needs

"There is no such thing as reproduction. When two people decide to have a baby, they engage in an act of production, and the widespread use of the word *reproduction* for this activity, with its implication that two people are braiding themselves together, is but a euphemism to comfort prospective parents before they get in over their heads."

"Far From The Tree" is a weighty book of almost 1,000 pages that begins with that fascinating sentence. In twelve compelling chapters and 300 pages of notes and resources, National Book Award-winning author Andrew Solomon dissects in fascinating detail the stories and special needs of children who are born with or develop disabilities: deaf; as dwarfs; with Down Syndrome, autism, or schizophrenia. He discusses the particular problems of parents whose children commit crimes, as well as child prodigies, sexual orientation and transgender issues and even children born of rape.

In the first chapter, *Son*, Mr. Solomon expands on his thoughts of "reproduction" as follows:

"In the subconscious fantasies that make conception look so alluring, it is often ourselves that we would like to see live forever, not someone with a personality of his own. Having anticipated the onward march of our selfish genes, many of us are unprepared for children who present unfamiliar needs. Parenthood abruptly catapults us into a permanent relationship with a stranger, and the more alien the stranger, the stronger the whiff of negativity. We depend on the guarantee in our children's faces that we will not die. Children whose defining quality annihilates that fantasy of immortality are a particular insult; we must love them for themselves, and not for the best of ourselves in them, and that is a great deal harder to do."

We don't intend to review *Far From the Tree* in this chapter but rather recommend it as a splendid resource for parents and professionals dealing with children with different needs. Mr. Solomon's personal experience, so eloquently told, gives greater meaning to his work.

"I had dyslexia as a child; indeed, I have it now. I still cannot write by hand without focusing on each letter as I form it, and even when I do, some letters are out of order or omitted.

"In 1993, I was assigned to investigate Deaf culture for the *New York Times*. My assumption about deafness was that it was a deficit and nothing more. Over the months that followed I found myself drawn into the Deaf world. Most deaf children are born to hearing parents, and those parents frequently prioritize functioning in the hearing world, expending enormous energy on oral speech and lipreading. Doing so, they can neglect other areas of their children's education. While some deaf people are good at lipreading and produce comprehensive speech, many do not have that skill, and years go by as they sit endlessly with audiologists and speech pathologists instead of learning history and mathematic and philosophy. Many stumble upon Deaf identity in adolescence, and it comes as a great liberation. They move into a world that validates Sign as a language and discover themselves. Some hearing parents accept this powerful new development; other struggle against it.

"The whole situation felt arrestingly familiar to me because I am gay. Gay people usually grow up under the purview of straight parents who feel that their children would be better off straight and sometimes torment them by pressing them to conform. Those gay people often discover gay identify in adolescence or afterward, finding great relief there…

"Then a friend had a daughter who was a dwarf. She wondered whether she should bring up her daughter to consider herself just like everyone else, only shorter; whether she should make sure her daughter had dwarf role models; or whether she should investigate surgical limb-lengthening. As she narrated her bafflement, I saw a familiar pattern. I had been startled to note my common ground with the Deaf, and now I was identifying with a dwarf; I wondered who else was out there waiting to join our gladsome throng. I thought that if gayness, an identity, could grow out of homosexuality, an illness, and Deafness, an identity, could grow out of deafness, an illness, and if dwarfism as an identity could emerge from an apparent disability, then there must be many other categories in this awkward interstitial territory. It was a radicalising insight."

Describing his own experience again:

"People ask when I knew I was gay, and I wonder what that knowledge entails. It took some time for me to become aware of my sexual desires. The realization that what I wanted was exotic, and out of step with the majority; came so early that I cannot remember a time preceding it. Recent studies have shown that as early as age two, male children who will grow up to be gay are averse to certain types of rough-and-tumble play; by age six, most will behave in obviously gender-nonconforming ways.

"I was popular at home, but I was subject to corrections. My mother, my brother, and I were at Indian Walk Shoes when I was seven, and as we were leaving, the salesman asked what color balloons we'd like. My brother wanted a red balloon. I wanted a pink one. My mother countered that I didn't want a pink balloon and reminded me that my favorite color was blue. I said I really wanted the pink, but under her glare, I took the blue one. That my favorite color is blue but I am still gay is evidence of both my mother's influence and its limits."

The coparenting point of these and other examples is simple to state but hard to achieve. A child with different needs requires co-parents to try even harder to get on the same page. Co-parents who magnify or intensify the conflict between them risk long-lasting damage to their special children. Co-parents should not only act in their child's best interest. They should strive for mutual understanding, for consistency and for respect.

Guardians ad litem sometimes have gay children in their cases, as well as a transgender adolescents, or transgender parents, dad to "mom and mommy." Often, the divorced parents succeed in working together to gain understanding and acceptance of their child's needs. In the one exception, the transgender child, the father bent over backwards—too far perhaps—to accept without hesitation his 12-year-old daughter's decision to live life as a boy, while the mother essentially disowned her after publicly insulting the child in a crowded restaurant.

Coparenting children with different needs is similar to the Covid-19 experience: It brings out the best intentions in most co-parents, and the worst in a few very high conflict cases. Perhaps the early intervention of therapists and other professionals who specialize in the area is what makes the difference. Not only the therapy and professional advice, but good therapists strive to get the parents on the same page by seeing them together or, if schedules do not permit that, by having a parent phone in during the session. Good therapists re-direct any anger and criticism from co-parents to the child's immediate needs and best interest. Most of them actively attempt to diffuse conflict as they search for common ground.

Close friends and relatives should be carefully vetted. Many will line up more eagerly to take sides in the case of divorced parents of children with different needs. If they have the best interest of the child in mind, this can be helpful. Or if they have specialized experience. However, if they are just choosing sides, it only adds to the conflict. Grandparents generally serve very well. Perhaps because of age, experience or a detachment from the parental role, grandparents give good advice to co-parents and a heap of unconditional love to their grandchildren.

Lisa: In the 2017 film based on Robert Solomon's book, directed by Rachel Dretzin, we see *Far From The Tree* come alive in documentary form. This film provides acknowledgment that parenting is especially difficult with children with unique differences. The complexity of addressing the needs of children with atypical learning differences, complicated physical, mental health or behavioral challenges, complex communication problems, gender or sexuality identity challenges, or other differences comes to the screen with all of the challenges and resilience that unique individuals and their families experience. This film is highly recommended for viewing by every family.

Each child is a unique individual. All children have their own abilities, challenges and gifts. Loving our children means accepting them and their uniqueness. This sounds like it should be easy and that we should all be able to do this easily but in fact, it is much more complicated than that. Our natural love for our children enables us to have empathy for their feelings and experiences. That does not mean that the parent-child relationship and the family level experiences will be easy or natural for us. It is important that families seek support when their parent-child relationship feels strained or when there is noticeable conflict, difficulty or challenges in the well-being of the child, parent or family system. Therapy can help us process the deep emotional responses that come with difficult life experiences. We gain support, guidance and insight from the therapeutic process at the same time as we allow ourselves to refocus our efforts on strengthening our relationships for healthy family interactions and well-being.

Chapter 27
Only Children

Guardians ad litem and therapists realize that only children experience different and sometimes more troubling problems when their parents divorce. That is the case in true *only* children as well as those children with older adult siblings or step siblings who have left home. Middle children can also feel like only children, stuck between a super smart, mature older sibling and a cute, adored younger child. This chapter covers them all.

Only children can seem shy, with a reticence to confide and a strong loyalty to one parent or another. Take, for example, 10-year-old Jason. He had been going back and forth between his divorced parents for two years with no apparent problems. Then he told his mother about the "funny, skinny cigarettes" his dad smoked, that "smelled weird," and the pictures he saw on his dad's cell phone that "freaked me out." Based on her past experience, the mother suspected marijuana and pornography. Although the father denied both, she suspended his timesharing with Jason. When their two lawyers got involved, a guardian ad litem was appointed to talk to Jason.

Irene: Jason's experience was his alone. If he'd had an older brother or sister, he could have confided in them, sought their advice. If he'd had younger siblings, his need to protect them might have come first. Alone, he was torn between betraying his father by talking to me or disappointing his mother after telling her his concerns. It took a few meetings alone with Jason to gain his trust. At his mother's home we played with his two dogs, throwing rubbers bones to them in the back yard. We "fished" for largemouth bass on a Play Station game connected to a large TV. Jason gave me the remote to "cast" under the large rocks in the river and feel the tension when I got a bite! We shared some fresh baked brownies alone on the patio. He still didn't want to talk to me about what bothered him. I arranged a brief visit for him to his father's home and watched him give his father a big hug but quickly walk away to perch on his grandfather's lap. He wouldn't even sit alone with me there.

It took another round of Play Station fishing before he said he wanted to tell me something "but it's too embarrassing and I can't say the words." He said it had to do with his father's cell phone. He went into another room, grabbed a pen, wrote "Naked People" in big letters on scrap paper and gave it to me. He opened up after that and we had a good talk. This was an easier case to solve as his father confessed, deleted the pictures from him phone, promised to keep it locked, swore off the marijuana and agreed to random drug testing. His timesharing with Jason was restored and Jason was happy to be with him again.

In a more difficult, very high conflict case involving Toby, a four-year-old boy, every decision either parent made became a contest, a battle of wills between them. Nightly bedtime rituals on Face Time for Toby with the absent parent were monitored and abused to the extent that Toby was lost in the process which became heated arguments between his parents. Toby's pre-K teacher found herself drawn into the conflict. Toby's pediatrician was cross examined about her recommendations regarding his allergies. *Both* parents thrived on the conflict, it seemed to me. If only Toby had siblings, both to provide a distraction for him, some empathy with the situation, but also to take his parents' focus off him, to diffuse their hostility. It's tough to be an only child in this situation.

Michelle Donley, Licensed Clinical Social Worker at the Costello Center in St. Petersburg, is a therapist skilled in working with only children caught between divorcing parents. She uses many techniques including play therapy with younger children to let them express their feelings indirectly, imaginatively.

"Only children are more aware and more tuned into family dynamics," Michelle told me. "They are more involved in emotional attention and loyalty issues. It's the Raggedy Ann syndrome as they are torn back and forth between parents—worse if one is an unhealthy parent.

"Siblings run in a pack. They team up, stick together. They often use code words or signals to diffuse the situation. The older siblings take responsibility for the others."

This, of course, can make things more difficult for older siblings. However, I have been amazed at how often this occurs and how well the older children accept this responsibility. Perhaps it distracts from their own hurtful feelings. I'm thinking particularly of 18-year-olds, no longer subject to timesharing orders, electing to go along with their younger siblings "to protect them," they tell me—regardless of whether those children really need "protection."

As I think back on it, I realize I've really enjoyed these sessions with only children, perhaps because once they open up to me, we have a special rapport and there is a sense of relief on their part, finally being able to share bottled up memories and feelings without the guilt of betrayal yet knowing action will be taken. It goes without saying that co-parents of only children must be super sensitive to the Raggedy Ann effect of their conflict.

Lisa: The shared experiences of siblings creates a strong and long-lasting bond. This is true whether those experiences are positive and joyful or stressful and painful. We always look to the unique individual needs of each child but when we see a sibling group we understand that there is a level of support between siblings that grow up together and experience the same family dynamics and experiences. Where does this leave only children? It leaves them alone. Alone in their suffering, their confusion, their grief and pain. With all eyes turned to the only child it also leaves them caught in the middle, feeling alone, responsible, and guilty.

We have talked about the profound sense of responsibility that children feel for their parents' conflict over them. When we consider the only child, this is amplified and creates a sense of self-blame, isolation, and distress for only children that often takes a lifetime to heal. Focused attention on how to buffer the impact of separation, divorce and parental conflict on only children needs to be the top priority for all parties. This means attending to the ways that children blame themselves for their parents' conflict and choices, understanding each child's unique needs, addressing the isolation and subsequent depression and anxiety that only children may experience and bringing in supportive mental health professionals. A child therapist with experience working with children in high conflict custody cases can help make an unbearable situation bearable. Professional help to assist in processing the grief, pain, loss, and loneliness experienced by only children during a divorce supports the child's emotional and mental health in deep ways that can change a child's life trajectory. It is never too soon, too late, or seemingly unnecessary to engage in therapy during difficult life experiences. In the case of only children and conflictual divorces, it is lifesaving.

Chapter 28
What Were You Thinking?

Parents, you are leaving huge footprints with your angry, hastily written, emotional and repetitive text messages.

Guardians ad litem, therapists and family law judges, read thousands of text messages between co-parents expressing hostility, profanity, disrespect, refusal to cooperate, ignorance of the best interest of the child and contempt for the court and its orders. Their reaction is usually, what were you thinking? Did you think that the judges, the family therapists and the guardian's ad litem would be reading them? Did that matter? Would you have stopped? The temptation to type and transmit without a filter is so great. It is the new reality in family court.

In reading a chain of copied text messages between parents, the escalation into outright anger and name-calling is so obvious one wonders if one parent is intentionally baiting the other? Who falls for it? What were *both* these parents thinking?

Angry judges read aloud the blistering, smut-filled invective sent by text from one co-parent to another, in the hopes that humiliation will bring it to an end. Children cry after getting a hold of a parent's cell phone and reading the gutter language the children have been taught not to use. Older adolescents, mostly girls, think it's okay to belittle or bully their "frenemies" by text because they've read their parents messages to each other. What were these parents thinking?

Many parent coordinators and family therapists spend countless hours, at the parent's expense, teaching basic communication skills before addressing underlying psychological and emotional problems, simply to wean these parents off overuse of text messaging. What were these parents thinking?

There does not seem to be any thinking happening. That is the problem. What is happening involves feelings that are not easy to contain. When we are angry or hurt we experience intense emotional pain that often overwhelms us. Those feelings create physical and cognitive responses. Our bodies tighten and our stomachs churn. The parts of our brain that allow us to process higher level thoughts turns off and the feeling center in our midbrain turn on. The limbic system goes into overdrive while we experience the rush of emotions and our bodies become readied for fight, flight or freeze. This is where we need to start our real work.

We can learn to regulate and calm our bodies and our brains. Self-regulation is an important skill that we begin developing at birth with thumb sucking and continue to develop throughout life. Some people have better self-regulation skills than others. Like all human behavior, if we want to be good at something we must learn how to do it and then practice it. We are all capable of thoughtful responses that promote positive communication.

The first step is deciding that we want to reduce the conflict in our relationships. That we believe that our lives will be better, happier and more joyful if we change the hostility in our communication to cooperation. We must acknowledge that our children are being terribly hurt by the negativity and conflict in the relationships and that they are worth changing for. If we can't do it for ourselves, we must do it for our children.

In Part IV, Some Solutions, you will find some helpful strategies for creating meaningful change in your coparenting relationship. The choice to change is yours, but the outcome of that change is not only yours it is also your children's and your children's children. Setting the tone for healthy relationships in your life and in the lives of your children starts with you and the relationship that you have with your co-parent. Let's look at solutions to conflict and ways to create more positive, less conflictual communication between you and your co-parent.

Chapter 29
It's Not Equal! It's Not "Fair."

Co-parents often complain that events involving their children "aren't equal" or "aren't fair." Here are several common situations:

1. Jen and Patrick put each other through college and graduate school, working part time jobs and raising a lovely daughter, Megan. The stress of their new jobs and trying to pay tuition for Megan's private elementary school finally got to them, and they divorced. It was amicable, they shared Megan 50/50 as she rotated between their apartments which were near to each other. Then Patrick's parents died in a tragic car accident. As their only heir, Patrick inherited their home in the suburbs and over two million dollars. Suddenly, there were no problems paying Megan's tuition, but the contrast between Jen's small apartment and Patrick's spacious home and pool gnawed at Jen. Megan raved about the sleepovers she could have with her friends at that home, the pool parties and the new clothes that Patrick bought her. Jen found herself sharp with Megan, telling her to "change the subject" or even just to "shut up." Jen worried that it "wasn't equal …wasn't fair." It began to eat away at her and Megan complained that "mom is mean to me."
2. Charlie remembered being surprised to find out his parents were never married as they lived together until he was ten and they got along so well. Then his mother fell in love with Ethan. Charlie was the "best man" at their wedding, which made him so happy, and a year later newborn twin girls made Charlie feel like a proud older brother. Everyone was happy, except for Seth, Charlie's father. He told Charlie he felt "completely cut out of your new life." Seth got angry with Charlie when he tried to show him pictures of the twins on his cell phone. Charlie and

Seth became estranged. It wasn't fun any longer to be together. Seth wept to his therapist: "It isn't equal…it isn't fair."

3. Maria and Frank were married two years after she crossed the U.S. border illegally, arriving from Guatemala. Frank worked for immigration services. Once he met the small, vivacious, dark-haired beauty, he had eyes for no other. He taught her to speak English, got her a green card, then married her, moved her into his house and helped her to learn all the customs and habits of her new country. Marie depended on him for everything and insisted on naming their son Frank Jr. Marie wanted to be a "stay at home mom," with Frank, Jr, and in fact she'd never held a job in the United States. She adored Frank Jr and began to withdraw from his father, rarely leaving the home and assigning all the shopping chores to Frank Sr. She wasn't interested in Frank Sr.'s activities or friends and the marriage deteriorated.

In the divorce, they agreed to equal timesharing. The marriage was too short for Maria to claim alimony. Frank paid hefty child support to Maria and bought her a new car, urging her to take driver's license and become more independent. He moved into an upscale apartment complex and began to date women he met online. Maria felt isolated and helpless. She had no real friends and was afraid to drive the new car. She told Frank Jr's kindergarten teacher that she had depended on her husband "for everything. I can't do it alone," she wailed. "It isn't equal. It isn't fair."

But Wait! Is It Ever Equal? Is It Ever Fair?

Life is never totally equal or totally fair. As adults we learn that things don't have to be equal to be fair and that things aren't necessarily fair if they are equal. So why do we have such a difficult time managing our expectations around everything being "equal or fair" when we separate or divorce? Parents agree that they are no longer happy with each other and then choose a path to separate and divorce. This choice creates an automatic division in what was once a life together that cannot possibly be split exactly equally. It ultimately leads to two separate lives, unequal in many ways.

No matter what the inequalities are after a split, each parent will need to pursue their own path and make their own life. One will make more money than the other, one will have more "stuff" than the other, one will have a bigger home than the other. Does this matter to how we raise our children and the quality of the parent-child relationship? Sometimes it does, but it should not. It actually creates opportunities for parents to concentrate on the important things with their children. Don't we need change to remind our children that every family is different, that their relationship with each parent is different and special in its own way? That each family and each parent and each home has its own special place in the life of the child? Can we put our own egos aside and think about how important it is for each child to have a unique and special relationship with each parent? It is up to co-parents to decide that it isn't going to be a competition.

Children want and need to tell each parent about life with the other parent. While such a simple concept, it is often misinterpreted by the parent receiving the information. Children want and need to share their lives with both of the parents that they love. No one can separate two totally different lives in two totally different families, especially not a child. Children want to share their feelings, thoughts and experiences with both parents. They may be happy to share new, fun or interesting things about their time with their other parent. They may want to share feelings of excitement, joy, and love from one house to the other, or, they may want to share feelings apprehension, fear or anger about the experiences they are having with the other parent. It is important that each parent put aside personal feelings and allow their child to be fully known, fully heard and fully safe with both parents.

In scenario #1 above, Jen could work through her own issues and feelings with a friend or therapist so that she is prepared to give Megan the support she needs with the following response: "I am so glad that you are having such a great time at your father's place. It is really cool that you get to enjoy some new and different things when you visit him". That's the response that Megan needs and wants. Jen has to figure out how to deal with her own feelings of jealousy and resentment so that she can be the parent that Megan needs her to be.

In scenario #2 above, Seth needs to process his complex feelings of sadness, resentment, and jealousy over the new life that Charlie is experiencing with new siblings. Seth needs to do his own emotional work with a therapist so that he is ready to support Charlie with the following response: "Charlie, it's awesome that you have new sisters, what a gift for you to have new little babies to love. I'm so happy for you, you're going to be the best big brother ever!" That's what Charlie needs to hear from dad.

In scenario #3, we are reminded that marriage and divorce is never equal and never fair. We all bring different knowledge, assets, skills, and capacities into the marriage with us. When the marriages end, we often leave with what we brought in and not much else. This won't always be fair or feel fair, but this is life. No one ever told us that life would be fair, and usually it is not. In this scenario it is important that Maria seeks out resources in her community to help her prepare for a more independent life. This would include going to a therapist to work on issues around self-esteem, distress or fear of isolation, anxiety, and re-entering her community in an empowered manner.

Divorce isn't easy, coparenting isn't easy but we can make it through and come out Ok on the other side. Remember, if we are okay, our children will be okay. While it may not seem equal or may not seem fair, if we focus on the best interest of our children it will be okay.

Bonus Chapter:
Been There, Done That: "Soapbox Musings from A Family Law Judge"

Been There, Done That: "Soapbox Musings from a Family Law Judge"

Judge Elizabeth Jack: When my friend Lisa Negrini asked me to write a chapter for her book, she did not give me a lot of details. I knew she was partnering with a retired judge well-known to me who often works as a guardian ad litem to write about children and divorce. Lisa asked me to write from the heart about my personal experiences.

"Divorcing with children." An overwhelming topic… where to begin? It feels like being asked to write an essay on "attending college." Or "traveling." But writing from the heart? I can do that. Let's see where my heart leads us.

A little history. I'm an attorney, a former prosecutor, working as a family law judge. I have two children, ages 17 and 19. I am divorced. I met my ex-husband as a college student at age 20, and not a very emotionally mature 20. We quickly became an item, and I was "all in" for being his partner for the next 17 years. At age 37, I began having some physical and emotional health issues that led to a healing journey resulting in my "waking up." For the 17 years I was with my ex-husband, I truly thought I could make the relationship work. When I woke up, I realized I could not. That year, 2007, when my children were 3 and 5 years old, began a litigation process that lasted for many years.

While I never practiced family law, I have jokingly said I earned a self-taught and self-awarded PhD in high-conflict divorce. I read every book and article I could get my hands on about high-conflict divorce with kids, and I attended intensive family law mediation and parenting coordination trainings. Finding it very difficult to co-parent with my ex-husband, I went back to school for psychology, thinking I would earn my masters and then PhD to develop evidence-based interventions to improve the family dynamics that lead to dysfunction in divorce cases. On the side, I explored opening a family law practice specializing in parenting coordination, with the goal being to heal families and "fix" the family law system so that it would overcome the root causes of conflict in divorcing families. Are you laughing? I am, looking back. While well-intentioned, this was a rather ambitious goal for one person to accomplish given that human beings were involved. Frustrated, and feeling like I had learned all I could to help my own family, I went back to prosecuting. Dealing with criminals and victims felt a lot less stressful than high-conflict divorce.

Fast-forward many years, now a family law judge, I have approximately 1200 cases assigned to me; not all of those are litigated. I only see the dynamics of the subset of cases that are litigated cases. Many parents figure out how to successfully form a new coparenting partnership without litigation. Or do they? Come to think of it, my divorce case involved a lot of stressful activity under the water (picture a sunken ship teeming with sharks and eels and schools of fish) but on the surface the judge would have had only a hint that all was not amicable. As for the cases I don't see in Court, the parties may be as dysfunctional as co-parents as they were as partners in their marriage. It is difficult for me to picture the family where two emotionally healthy people who loved each other enough to start a family together decide to divorce merely because they aren't growing together or have simply fallen out of love. Not being one of those people during my divorce, I would guess those people stay together, but perhaps not. Regardless, my musings are from my own experience and the subset of cases that I see.

In some cases, there is a lot of conflict at the beginning of the divorce process, and then it calms down. Other cases involve frequent flyers who come to court repeatedly during the divorce and for years afterwards. My judicial philosophy is that when conflict arises, get the parents in quickly and try to come up with a case management plan so everyone knows what to expect. I believe that the mere fact of having a plan will ease anxiety and help calm down the conflict. Often, that works. But not always.

I have heard that in family law approximately 20 percent of divorce cases with children become high conflict, and that within that group, approximately 80 percent are cases in which one or both parents have a personality disorder. If true, this could explain why I see certain cases over and over again, while other cases (with healthier parties) calm down and the family seems to move forward after the initial storm.

Like most of us, I have many friends with children who are now separated, divorced, or divorcing who ask me for my thoughts. And of course, I am in court every day with such people. As a result, I have developed what I call my "Soapbox Musings." I have an assortment of speeches, specially selected for the circumstances or what I feel is going on with a family. Clearly, not all of my musings are right for every family. I mix and match the details within them. Below is an assortment of my musings, grouped by general topic but in no ways an exhaustive or perfectly organized list.

Finally, a disclaimer. Giving advice in this area makes me a little nervous. During my divorce, I was so ungrounded and desperate for guidance that I treated every suggestion as gospel, sometimes with results the complete opposite of those intended. Words only have the meaning that we as the listener bring to them. So please, take my musings with many grains of salt. Perhaps you will hear things that help you, or that you discard as rubbish. That is fine, and in fact, strongly recommended.

(A note about the terms used: I use the term "divorced" when many of my cases involve parents who never married. I also speak about living arrangements as if the pattern is always a couple who once lived together as partners and now are trying to co-parent in two homes. In reality, I see a wide variety of family situations. Please understand that my messages are meant to be broader than the terms used, and that the terms were chosen merely for simplicity's sake.)

Lower Your Expectations. The System Isn't Perfect, So Don't Expect It to Be.

Family law is rooted in a system of advocacy that is thousands of years old, where citizens hire others to fight for their positions. This system lifts families in the heat of a crisis and lays them onto a cold framework of laws to spit out hugely impactful decisions. Despite the obvious challenges to getting such a system perfectly right, I truly think Florida has done as good a job as can be expected to honor our nation's chosen system of advocacy while trying to reach helpful outcomes for families in the midst of highly emotional interpersonal disputes.

However, given that human beings are involved, there can be no "perfect" system or outcome. There are just too many variables and nuances. Of course, each player's unique character traits will greatly affect how a case proceeds. Family lawyers bring their own personalities to the table, with different philosophies and varying levels of experience and creativity. A lawyer may naturally be a fierce advocate who likes to fight out disagreements, or perhaps is a highly effective peace-seeker. The lawyers' and parties' personalities will greatly affect the various disputes that arise within a case, and/or the overall outcome of a case. What happens in your case is just one permutation of a huge combination of possibilities. Don't expect that the system and process will get everything "right" from your perspective.

And, oh yes, the judge assigned may also have an effect.

Judges Are Not Computers. Your Case May Be Affected By the Judge Assigned.

A seasoned judge I know refers to the "therapeutic justice" of family law, and reminds junior judges that to be effective, we must be creative problem solvers. Notwithstanding the fluidity of a family law judge's role in a case, all judges must follow the law. Florida statutes set forth various factors for deciding family law cases such as the "best interest of a child" factors that must be considered for any parenting plan that is approved or decided by a judge. I have a friend who works in technology who went through a high-conflict divorce; he thinks the best interest factors should be put into a computer and the computer should spit out the result. If only it were that simple. (And fortunately, it is not, or I would be out of a job!)

Perhaps more so than other areas of law, family law necessarily requires judges to draw upon their life experiences and value systems to make decisions. In family law, the jury is replaced with the judge as the fact-finder. Your judge will be randomly assigned. Does your judge believe that a parenting plan should be followed even if a parent believes a child is being emotionally traumatized by following the plan? Is your judge inclined to believe that any withholding of a child is likely the result of parental alienation and rule accordingly? As a colleague recently reflected while discussing a difficult contempt motion, "Just think, two judges can each hear the same evidence, both follow the law, reach totally different results, and neither of them is legally wrong!"

Of course, there are situations where the law dictates a very specific result; but when facts are involved and credibility determinations must be made, not all fact-finders will reach the same conclusions. The judge's case management style may also play a role; does the judge like to manage the case at the first sign of conflict, or wish to discourage litigation and have the parties work out their differences by being as uninvolved as possible? Your assigned judge will be another unique factor that may greatly affect the trajectory of your case as well as the outcomes of disputed issues. This is one more reason to try to resolve your differences on your own, as discussed below.

Your Co-parent Is Equally Your Child's Parent.

Back when I was going to fix family law, I read an excellent article in a psychology journal on the topic of "what is in a child's best interest." The author pointed out that often in the family law context, we speak about "the best interest of a child" as if we are all speaking the same language; we are not. The author opined that unspoken differences in underlying values lay at the heart of many parenting disputes. For example, many people think the ability to see and meet a child's emotional needs is the most important factor in parenting. Some believe other aspects of child-rearing (such as providing discipline, structure, and routine) are most important. Adequate financial resources may be considered very important by some (i.e. a parent with greater resources can provide more educational options, travel experiences, and a healthier and more stimulating living environment.) [Note: Child support laws do work to allow each parent to provide basic support.]. None of those perspectives are right or wrong, just as none of us are perfect parents and none of our children are entitled to perfect parents. When divorcing parents cannot reach their own agreement about what is best for their child, the law merely requires that the child has "good enough" parents who can each provide enough "good stuff" to make sure the child is healthy and safe. The picture of ideal parenting that each parent would paint may look very different from the picture the other parent would paint.

Co-parents may be, and are encouraged to be, on the same page about certain things (i.e. no spanking, bedtime is at 8, or homework before playtime) but they very well may not be. Even parents who stay in committed relationships may find child-rearing to be a huge source of conflict. One can imagine that the personality differences that led to incompatibility as partners make it that much more difficult for divorced parents to co-parent well.

Some co-parents must learn to let go of micromanaging their co-parent's parenting decisions (absent safety concerns, of course.) Once you divorce, you likely will not get to decide who your co-parent hires as a babysitter, what he or she feeds your child for dinner, or whether he or she makes your child bathe every day. You may even have to let go of things that feel very important to you such as what time your toddler gets to preschool. Letting go can be extremely difficult for a parent who was the primary caregiver and child-issue decision-maker when married; such a parent may still have a lot of his or her identity wrapped up in that role. Such a parent must give his or her co-parent space to learn how to be a good enough parent. As for the parent who feels micromanaged? Try to have some compassion and be polite when discussing your boundaries, and try to not be hyperactive to advice from your co-parent; realize your co-parent is learning a new role as well.

New Partners Are Not Co-parents.

You and your former partner are the co-parents, and NOT you and your new partner as one, and your co-parent as the other. While new partners and stepparents can be a blessing, coparenting is not a "throuple." There are situations where a new partner provides critical support and assistance in special situations, such as providing supervision for a newly sober co-parent. However, co-parents who are getting along well may unexpectedly and suddenly experience conflict when a new partner enters the coparenting dynamic. The new relationship may bring more children, tighter finances, and new schedules to an already delicate balancing act. I urge the co-parent who has a new partner to honor the two-parent coparenting relationship with their ex-spouse and prioritize it over the complex evolving dynamics of a new blended family. As a result, some conflict may be avoided.

Children Really and Truly Are Resilient, and They Really and Truly Can Come Out of This OK.

We have all heard the expression, "children/babies are resilient." That may be true, but they need at least one grounded person in their lives who is able to see them, feel them, and understand their emotional needs. Think of a young child who starts elementary school with a stern teacher who is not a nurturer. A sensitive child may start the year in tears. But maybe the teacher is very good at academics and discipline, allowing for the students to gain a strong foundation in math and reading. The teacher's style and the environment may even give a sensitive child confidence and a sense of independence. That teacher is providing positive things, just not everything that child needs. That child may get to go home to a very soft and fuzzy home where their sensitivities are seen and heard and validated, and they get through the year just fine.

Children can swim in and out of different environments without being traumatized, and they often grow from doing so. Your home is going to give your child some things he or she needs, and your co-parent's home will do the same. Strive to see and hear your child when your child is with you, and trust that your support will often be enough to help them navigate the rest of their world. Note: When you see that your child is struggling, and you need outside help, don't hesitate to seek out a qualified children's mental health counselor who can help ease your child's stress and support their transitions.

Litigation Is Stressful. Try To Avoid It.

As I was navigating the litigation process myself, I recall feeling very stressed over routine daily tasks and decisions, as if the judge had a crystal ball (like the Wicked Witch in the Wizard of Oz) and every move I made would be a significant factor that would affect my litigation. For years, I was worried about planning a vacation, because I was afraid a court date might come up. My attorney reassured me the Court would work around a vacation, but then I worried that would just make the judge think I was not prioritizing the case and my children. When coparenting was at its worst, I was keeping notes and a log to document various coparenting issues just in case documentation was needed. It was crazy-making.

Uncertainty is stressful, in all aspects of life. Litigation about your children is uncertainty on steroids. Focusing on the litigation compounds the problem. If you can avoid litigation without sacrificing those things that cannot be sacrificed (and I can't tell you what those things are, only you know), I urge you to do so. Many of the smaller parenting plan issues that seem so important really are not, in the greater scheme of things.

You Can't See Your Children Until You See Yourself.

Before my separation, my then very young daughter was having some emotional issues that seemed to be related to men, and boys at her school. I reached out for professional help and was extremely offended when the therapist wanted to focus on me and my relationship with my ex-husband. Although I did not go back that therapist, I did start the divorce process less than a year later. I now realize (and know first-hand) that if you can plainly see that your child is suffering but you do not understand what it is causing their upset, most likely there is some cloudiness within you that is blocking your insight. Maybe your partner has some issues that you believe are causing some of your child's problems, but it was due to reasons within you that you chose that person for a partner. We pass a lot of our own baggage on to our children and until we fully understand ourselves, we cannot fully help our children. As a divorced older friend with children repeatedly told me while I was struggling at the end of marriage: There is a reason parents are told on a plane to put on their own oxygen masks before helping their children. If you don't know how to help your struggling child, turn within and get help for yourself; solutions for how to help your child will likely make themselves known to you.

Many of us have attachment issues that developed from being less than perfectly-parented as young children. If you were an unhealthy person in a dysfunctional marriage you may be immediately drawn to another (shiny and freshly-packaged) unhealthy relationship. Work on yourself enough that you are not dependent on a new relationship to be happy. Until we know ourselves, we repeat the same patterns. New unhealthy relationships will greatly add to the stress of divorcing and coparenting. Wait to date, if you can. If you can't, try to not go too fast. Take a break if you start to see old patterns in the new relationship. Do not worry that your kids will be damaged if you remove an unhealthy partner from their lives. They need and want YOU. (All to themselves whenever possible, if you haven't noticed.) They may tolerate someone new but if that person is shown the door, your kids are going to be just fine.

Put your children first. No, I mean it. Really and truly put them first. Saying "no" to unhealthy relationships and working on yourself IS putting your kids first.

You Can Only Control Yourself.

The person you are divorcing is the same person to whom you were married. For some reason, when I decided to divorce, I developed magical thinking that suddenly my ex-husband and I would get along beautifully and be on the same page about how to raise the children. (I even pictured us having Christmas breakfast together maybe with blended families while all the kids opened presents!) Yeah. That did not happen. Shocker. During the divorce and after, we were the same people we were when married, and the stress of litigation further entrenched us in our shortcomings as individuals and partners.

You cannot control the other person's self-awareness or growth. You cannot dictate how they will behave during or after the divorce. Stop thinking that you are controlling their behavior through your actions. You are not. You can only control yourself. Work on improving yourself, keep your own side of the street clean, and trust that good things will flow from that.

It May Need to Get Worse Before It Gets Better.

There are many types of families where sometimes the conflict has to get worse than it was in the marriage before things will get better. If you had a very dysfunctional marriage, with power and control issues, the dynamic may need to be shaken up for the parties to engage in a new way. If a more equal partnership is ever going to result, there may first need to be a great deal of conflict, possibly for the first time. Even with two relatively emotionally healthy parents, the stress of litigation, fears about financial insecurity, or resentments over changing roles or new partners, may create some initial conflict that later settles down. If there are personality disorders involved, the conflict may never settle down, but you will get stronger and develop skills to cope. Do not allow the fact of present conflict define how things will be in the future. The divorce process is a moment in time; once the conflict passes, move forward in a positive way.

A note about dysfunction: There can be dynamics that are subtle and covert, and hard to make visible. Yes, your children may be suffering some emotional harm. But at some point, you may need to accept that your children need to have their experience, and you cannot make the situation better for them. By fighting through litigation, you may be doing more harm than good. Built into your analysis of how to proceed should be the odds of getting what you want, and the harm that will come to your kids from acting or not acting. Not all professionals, or all people, are going to see and understand the situation.

Compromise

Getting divorced means not having your kids in your life all the time; suck it up buttercup and get used to it (spoken with love). You are probably not going to get everything you want. It almost always is better if the two co-parents can work things out for themselves. Of course, when parents can't work things out and I'm asked to make a decision, it isn't like I'm throwing a dart at a dartboard. My decisions are informed by what the parents are requesting. Imagine that the details of parenting plans are somewhere between A and Z. Often, the parents are aware that based on the facts of the case, my decision is probably going to land somewhere between J and Q. Having attorneys litigate between J and Q can be very expensive. And under the current state of the law, a judge is limited in the scope of the decision he or she may make; except in certain circumstances, a judge is limited to deciding a parenting plan based on the current age and situation of the child and the parties. A judge usually cannot factor in future events, even though we know children will grow, work schedules may adjust, and home situations may change as time passes.

The litigation process is stressful and takes time and energy away from your kids. Does the size of your disagreement with your co-parent really warrant the enormous expenditures that will be required to have a stranger, like me, make parenting decisions for you? Plus, litigating gives parties a forum in which to sling mud, which can exacerbate the problem and make it much harder to co-parent well in the future. The process of working out your differences as co-parents now can help you develop the skills you will need to get along to make all of the decisions you will be making together as your child gets older.

There are cases where one parent is seeking A and the other parent is seeking Z. Maybe there are serious safety concerns, and if one parent is not recognizing them (i.e. substance abuse, or mental health issues) there is no choice but to litigate. Other times there are relocation issues, where parents live far apart; this can be a very difficult issues for parents to resolve as it seems like there is no room for compromise. One parent necessarily must be the majority school-year timeshare parent. If the parents can afford it, the child may get to visit the other parent frequently but often this is not possible. Each parent may feel the urge to fight hard to provide the school year home. Set your egos aside. Would it really be impossible for you to maintain a strong relationship with your child if you are not the school-year parent? Can you visit your child for all of those big events? Can you have daily phone and video time, where your child shares about his or her day? Can you and your child enjoy wonderful quality time without the stress of school responsibilities? Of course you can! By not staying together, you and your co-parent created this difficult situation, and one of you is going to have to be the away parent. For long-distance co-parents, having the child only during vacation and holiday times can be a wonderful opportunity. You can work together to find a solution, or you can spend the equivalent of your child's college education using the advocacy system, where each parent points out their own strengths and the other's weaknesses, to have a randomly selected stranger (like me) make critically important decisions for your child and your family.

It can be hard on the ego to have to accept a public pronouncement that the other parent is the majority timeshare parent. (This may be exacerbated based on the sex of the parties.) A parent may think, "I must be, or seem to be, a terrible mother/parent if I only have 40% of my child's nights," even if that is what makes the most sense based on geography, or work schedules, or educational needs. Look into your heart and put the needs of your child first, ahead of your ego; by doing this, you will be the absolute best parent your child can have.

Your Family Is Unique.

Take all the advice you get with a grain of salt, for every family is unique. I wanted to do divorce so well. I got a lot of advice and took every word literally. I remember one family at the school where my children attended. They divorced so amicably that the parents and their new spouses would take vacations with all of their children together. Women's Day Magazine wrote a glowing article about their blended families. When these parents heard I was divorcing, one of them reached out to encourage me to get along with my children's father post-divorce. Doesn't that sound wonderful? (Again, visions of Christmas mornings… not sure why I am so fixated on Christmas morning as proof of successful coparenting, but I digress…). I wanted to be that cool couple, the poster children for how to divorce well. Again, shocker, that did not happen for me. And looking back, I think my attempts to keep things from getting unpleasant delayed the eventual explosion and painful process that had to occur before things could get better.

Your Family and Your Children Can Come Out Of This Process OK.

With divorce, your life may be upended and you may lose many of your friends, and even some family. Figuring out a new schedule and routine can be difficult and unsettling. Sometimes your children will be with you, and other times you will be completely alone. You are going through a period of adjustment. At the end of this process, if you approach it the right way, you will have grown in ways that will benefit your children. There are some benefits to divorcing when your children are younger, if that is the right choice for you and your family. You get to start the process of living a more authentic life, and in turn, your children will have the benefit of you raising them while being a more whole and healthier person.

I have friends going through divorce with older children, and the consequences of their life choices are now hitting them in the face. For the first time, they are asking themselves "who am I and what do I want?" They may struggle with breaking up the family, especially if their children were shielded from their marital unhappiness. Whenever it occurs, your divorce will present you with a huge opportunity to work on yourself for the benefit of your family. Don't get mired in the litigation part, especially if your children are young.

Children Feel Everything; Be an Example Through Your Actions.

There is an expression in the psychology world that "children swim in our unconscious minds." You may have heard stories about children who see spirits, or come into the world with past-life memories. By age 5 or 6, society has conditioned much of our extreme sensitivity to energy out of us. If you have young children, they are feeling everything going on inside of you. They know you are upset and stressed, and if your court case goes on for years, that is years of their childhood they will not get back.

Be an example to your children. If you can, show them that two loving parents can grow apart but still work together to put them first. Show them how much you love them by treating your co-parent well, very well. The rewards of your actions will pay off in your children's future relationships.

Cooperation, communication and compromise represent the pinnacle of coparenting success. But if that is not possible? Default to no conflict. No conflict is better than conflict. Are those exchanges where neither parent says a word stressful on kids? Yes, but even worse is when you are screaming obscenities at each other. If your other parent is not taking the high road, take the high road. Your children will always know what is really going on, they can feel it.

Children Want Both Parents in Their Lives; Honor That.

As a former prosecutor I know, even in abuse situations, children want both their parents in their lives, even when one or both of them are not healthy people. Every single one of us is dealt a hand of cards at birth. We may have great parents, academic skills, artistic talents, emotional intelligence, or some of us may be lucky enough to have several of these things. Some of us are born with dysfunctional parents. Children, just like all of us, deserve to have their experience and know their parents. They cannot and should not be shielded from reality.

You know that situation when you know in your gut things aren't right but you aren't getting any validation? Your kids also need that validation. A child may want to vent about your co-parent. Their safety valve should not be you. When your child vents to you about the other parent, you may feel the (well-intentioned but overly protective) need to address whatever issue the child is raising, thus adding fuel to your fire. Also, face it, whether you like it or not, you are biased. Give you child a space (such as with a counselor) where he or she can let off steam, have his or her feelings validated, and develop coping skills. Also, mental health professionals are mandated to report any concerns of abuse, which will take some weight off your worried shoulders.

For many reasons, parenting plans encourage and require parents to support the child's relationship with the other parent. Children have the right and the need to form their own opinions. Children deserve to know their parents, even unhealthy ones (with boundaries for safety, as needed). Even abused children crave connection with both parents on a basic biological level because for infants, rejection means death. Trust me on this—if your child perceives you as trying to keep them from knowing their other parent, they will perceive you as a threat and your child will no longer view you as that safe harbor he or she needs.

Don't Sweat The Small Stuff.

It can be infuriating to have clothes you purchased for your child disappear, and it may feel like a sign of disrespect. I have witnessed (through my Court cases) more conflict over the exchange of hair accessories than one person should in a lifetime. I do realize that when conflict is brewing, a hair bow feels like much more than a hair bow. Maybe one parent delivered the child to preschool on time all but 5 times in a year but is outraged their co-parent (who maybe lives further away, or has an infant too) got the child there late 12 times. Unless you are a perfect human being, co-parent, and parent (and I have yet to meet that person) you are holding your co-parent to an impossible standard and you are inviting conflict. I am not dismissing the importance of structure and routine for children; and, sometimes apparently smaller issues are part of a bigger pattern that ends up being a large part of a litigated case. But to the extent you can, let the little things go. It is extremely stressful and detrimental for your children to be in the midst of these battles.

Conclusion

I liken the divorce process to grieving. In many amicable divorce hearings where the parties have agreed to everything and are remaining friends, one or both parties start crying. (Even as the judge, I have felt my eyes welling up over the palpable pain.) Most of us get married and become parents believing our happiness will last forever. Even in the best divorce situations, it can be very difficult to accept that the dream is over. When children are involved, the loss and regret can feel almost unbearable.

If you got through my wandering ramblings, you may have noticed these musing have some common themes. Create a new dream. Imagine a life where you and your children are living healthy, whole and authentic lives, facing life's challenges with honesty and grace. Put your children first and know and heal yourself. Do these things and I promise; you and your children will be just fine.

Part IV
Some Solutions

Chapter 30
Some Practical Solutions – 10 Steps to Better Coparenting in a Digital World

1. Recognize the harm caused to your child by your behavior. Most parents are good people who want the best for their children; they just don't recognize the damage done. Children don't point it out to parents. They rely on parents to do the right thing. When parents don't, children suffer. Recognizing the harm is the first step.
2. Start talking to each other, preferably in person but if not by phone, about the little things. Small talk. Funny things the kids did. What their teachers say about them. Good grades or science projects, etc. Break the ice with these and tackling more difficult subjects will be easier.
3. Bring the children into a nice conversation between you. Hug them. Praise them. Laugh with them. "Let's talk to Dad about it" is a very good statement. It includes the child, the other parent, uses the word "talk" and creates hope.
4. If you are in litigation, and with due respect to good family law attorneys, find a family therapist, parent coordinator, mediator and/or a guardian ad litem as early as possible in your case.
5. Treat in-laws as an asset! You don't have to spend as much time with them, but as a co-parent you may need them as much as your own family. Respect them, and don't be afraid to ask for their help.
6. Practice feeling positive, speaking in compliments, smiling a lot. At the same time, don't hesitate to discipline your children when they need it.
7. Correct your child if he speaks disrespectfully about your co-parent or calls a co-parent by a first name. Your child will actually respect you for this.

8. Regarding phone calls and Face Time to a young child, remember that they have a short attention span and they care much less about the call than you do.
9. If you have scrapbooks, pictures or cell phone memories of better times with your co-parent, share them with your child. It makes the child very happy to learn of the good times.
10. Try renting a two-person kayak for a two-hour trip down a river or spring with your co-parent. You will find you cooperate well out of necessity!

Chapter 31
It Isn't Easy

Coparenting Does Not Happen Easily!

Coparenting requires a great deal of patience, forgiveness, flexibility and focus, focus, focus. If you focus on the best interest of your child, coparenting will be easier for you and your ex and your child. Even in cases where anger, animosity and anxiety are at high levels, those demons of destruction won't prevent good coparenting if you can keep your focus where it counts: On the best interest of your child.

Because parents love their children, they often instinctively know what is in their best interest. But roadblocks get in the way. Most of us are better giving advice to others than taking it ourselves. What advice would you give to these couples to improve their coparenting?

1. Cyndie and Todd hardly knew each other when they found out she was pregnant. Their emotions were mixed. Both regretted their post-happy hour tryst, but each of them wanted a child—they just didn't want each other. They were in their late thirties with established careers in hospital management. Cyndie knew she could support the child by herself. While still pregnant, Cyndie offered Todd a written agreement absolving him of all financial responsibility if he would waive all his parental rights. Todd was shocked, hurt and insulted. He refused to sign it. Instead, he was present for his son's birth and insisted on an immediate 50/50 time sharing arrangement. Strangers raising a child.

How can Cyndie and Todd ever Co-parent?

The answer is pretty obvious. They have to get to know each other, to learn to trust each other, as soon as possible, ideally during the pregnancy. With full time jobs, neither is going to be a stay-at-home parent so they should get to know each other's families or close friends likely to be used as caregivers. If day-care is necessary, they should visit the prospective day-care centers together. Cyndie and Todd should also take a parenting class *together,* so they hear the same advice. For time sharing problems, they might want to retain a parent coordinator, mediator or family therapist to help them work out the schedule.

Regardless of which resources they choose, by being proactive, coparenting can begin on the right foot. Even before the birth of their child, Cyndie and Todd can learn to co-parent respectfully. A positive start bodes well for the next eighteen years.

2. Richard and Emily were high school sweethearts who worked hard to put each other through college while raising two children, born a year apart. Their busy lives were family centered. Both wanted the best for their children, more than their parents had been able to provide for them. Emily taught science at a private school that paid little in salary but waived tuition for her children to attend. She had summers off and time after school to be with the children. Richard climbed the corporate ladder at a national executive recruiting firm. He worked long hours for a growing income that allowed for a lovely home with a big mortgage, club membership, tennis and golf lessons and expensive summer camps for the children. Richard traveled a lot for work and left the home and childcare to Emily. He kept in touch with the family electronically, by Facetime and text messages, as well as Sunday outings when he was home and expensive summer vacations for the family. Although they spent less time with their father, the children loved both parents and the arrangement seemed workable, until Richard began an affair with Tracy, a younger colleague. He asked Emily for a divorce and for equal time sharing with the children, now nine and ten years old. Shell shocked, Emily retained an expensive divorce lawyer and hit Richard with a claim for permanent alimony and the family home.

The coparenting problem in this case is that the children's issues, including time sharing, activities and support, may be held hostage while litigating financial matters. Children feel the stress and anxiety their parents experience during the litigation. It's impossible for the children to escape it.

The solution is to carve out issues involving the children and begin family therapy as soon as possible. A skilled family therapist can help the children deal with the surprise of their parents' divorce while helping the parents create a parenting plan, time sharing schedule and effective communication even during the litigation. It isn't easy. Emily is heartbroken and Richard feels she is taking him to the cleaners. However, family therapy is in the best interest of their children and both Emily and Richard want that.

There is almost no good reason to postpone timesharing and coparenting issues. They should be resolved as soon as possible, even if financial and property matters need to be litigated.

3. Stacy and Clark have five children between them, one from their own relationship and two each as a result of "blending" their families six years ago. Stacy is technically just the "stepmother" to Clark's two teenage girls because their biological mother who rarely sees them and doesn't pay support wouldn't let her adopt them. Clark, however, did adopt Stacy's two boys as their biological father's rights were terminated when he was sentenced to prison for child abuse. The children range in ages from sixteen down to three years old.

Stacy and Clark met online while both were working two jobs and struggling to raise their children on their own. They had a few dates together in local bars and agreed to rent a house together big enough for the seven of them. Their friends knew of their financial struggles and combined to throw a big "housewarming" party for them, which Stacy and Clark decided to turn into a surprise wedding. A year after the marriage their son was born.

Family life was chaotic from the beginning. Stacy's two boys, now in middle school, suffered from untreated post-traumatic stress caused by their biological father's abuse. Stacy was reluctant to discipline them when needed. Although Clark had adopted the boys, he didn't want any part of the discipline. Understandably, the boys were wild at home and in school. Clark's girls, on the other hand, loved having Stacy as a female figure they lacked, but resented the extra household chores and especially the babysitting. Stacy began to hide bottles of vodka and retreat to a locked bedroom to escape the chaos after work. Clark grew frustrated with the added responsibility caused by Stacy's drinking and he became addicted to pornography online and to frequent visits to strip clubs.

It wasn't long before both grandmothers and the couple's friends realized the children were raising themselves. Stacy and Clark had lost all respect for each other. Divorce was inevitable. Clark's mother paid a retainer to an attorney for her son. Stacy obtained her lawyer through legal aid. The family law judge exclaimed that the case was a mess.

What can this family do? What will happen to these children? This remains a family law case and not a child protection case in dependency court, mainly because of the intervention by the grandmothers and friends, as well as the help of the teenage girls. But the case is hugely complicated because of the trauma suffered by all these children past and present—the previous losses in their lives, the lack of discipline and parental responsibility, and the addictions of Stacy and Clark. The lawyers are merely bandaids in this case. What is first needed is a professional who can talk to all the children in the home, someone who can be their voice and tell the family court judge what they need in the way of therapy, and what is in their best interest going forward regarding time to be spent with each parent. A good first step is for the Court to appoint a guardian ad litem – a family lawyer or perhaps a psychologist – who can be the voice of these children in court and who can recommend various therapies and eventually a reasonable parenting plan in the divorce.

It isn't easy, but there are resources at hand. The expense is almost always worth it if litigation and resulting stress and anxiety are reduced.

Chapter 32
The Chicago Judges

Bob Downs, the former president of the Illinois State Bar Association, currently practices family law in Oak Park, a close suburb of Chicago. We reached out to Bob to put together a think tank of experienced family law judges and guardians ad litem in Chicago. The purpose was to broaden our search for solutions in high conflict family law cases—solutions that might improve communication between parents of children caught in the middle of the struggle.

Judge Grace Dickler, presiding judge of the domestic relations division, convened the meeting and Judge Karen Bowes graciously allowed us to use her courtroom for a working lunch. Judges Gregory Ahern, Edward Arce, Karen Bowes, Jeanne Cleveland-Bernstein, Renee Goldfarb, Robert Johnson, Mark Lopez, Martha Sullivan and Debra Walker joined us, as well as guardians ad litem David Wessel and Robert Ackley.

The session began with skepticism that any real solutions could be found. The judges quickly reached a consensus that parents in Chicago's high conflict cases were no different or less challenged than parents anywhere else in the country. They agreed right away that lawyers often mirror their client's personality and can stoke the animosity. But, as conversation flowed and specific ideas that worked percolated upwards, the atmosphere got more optimistic.

Judge Walker immediately pointed out that high conflicts are "pervasive, rich and poor alike, not related to social or economic status." As soon as she senses conflict and hostility, Judge Walker said she asks the parents what they want for their child. "Do you want your child to be healthy, to be able to communicate and to have healthy relationships? This often works. By emphasizing the child, I feel I've made a little difference in the case."

"At first they're not listening to me," Judge Cleveland-Bernstein added. "They want to throw barbs at each other. They're not listening to the law. The law goes right over them." She said "I tell this to them: 'The child loves his mother, loves his father. If you say to the child your father hurt me or your mother is a bitch and only cares about the money, what does that do to the child, for he is just like mother and just like father. Those words hurt him terribly and parents *will* listen when you talk about their children."

Judge Lopez approaches it a different way. "If something should happen to you, I tell them, the other parent will be raising your child. Therefore, it is important to be respectful of that person." The judge compared divorced situations to more transitory relationships with children. "Anyone who is getting divorced has had a structure of some sort, not like a one-night stand where there is little knowledge of each other or living together or structure. Those relationships are really difficult."

Guardian Ad Litem David Wessel was the first to mention lawyers and most of the judges nodded in agreement. "Lawyers often mirror their clients' personalities as well as the animosity. If there is no communication between their lawyers, you can bet there is no communication between the parents. Family law judges have a very important role in setting the right tone. They shouldn't let anyone say the word 'liar' in their courtroom."

Attorney Bob Downs picked up on this thought. In his term as president of the Illinois bar, he chose the theme "The Role of the Bench in the Civility of Lawyers." He told our group that "civility in family law is most important because a larger section of ordinary people is affected. Judges can play a greater role than they do in altering the behavior of attorneys." Like Mr. Wessel, Mr. Downs serves as a guardian ad litem in Cook County, which "has the largest unified court system in the world, with more than 400 judges." He criticized the long-standing practice of "using domestic relations as a dumping ground for judges. It is too important for that."

Judge Walker had another technique for reducing the conflict. "I talk about the future," he said, "those fabulous days of high school and college graduations, weddings and grandchildren. Parents in conflict can be dug into the past or the present. If I can make them think about the future, years after the case is over, they begin to smile." Mr. Wessel made the point that "often the reason for the divorce is that the couple can't communicate. Then we expect them to resolve problems while in court with litigation? There has to be a way to put the onus on the lawyers to problem solve."

Sometimes a little humor can drive the point home, Judge Martha Sullivan said. "During a divorce these folks are so focused on themselves. It's like they have blinders on. When a dad complained about his girlfriend, saying 'She got pregnant,' I asked him 'Really, all by herself?'"

Judge Bowes, who practiced family law before she took the bench, pointed out that many lawyers encourage their clients to communicate by e mail or text "because it creates a record they can use in court if needed. If timesharing is on Monday and the parent doesn't show up until Tuesday, a reminder by text can prove it." It is building the case, instead of fostering good communication.

Three of the judges mentioned mental illness as a complicating problem in family law. "Mental illness creates big problems," Judge Goldfarb said. "Substance abuse does too, but there is more treatment available for that." Judge Bowes described mental illness as "ranging from mild to barely functional. When we find a good therapist, we overwhelm them and pretty soon they can't serve anyone new."

When we asked for specific programs in Chicago that worked to diffuse conflict in family law, the judges had their own favorites. Judge Cleveland-Bernstein said "Chief Judge Dickler pulls the parties out of the system and sends them to early intervention, which is like mediation only court-based. Judge Bowes is a fan of family counseling. However sometimes kids are rushed into counseling and the therapist doesn't know the law. As a judge, I don't know therapy but when the therapist doesn't know the law it results in a recommendation like 'she doesn't have to go with her father unless she wants to.' That's not the law." Judge Goldfarb agreed. "Illinois law says the goal is maximum parenting contact. That's the law."

Guardian-ad-litem Wessel suggested the therapists should work as a team with the family, attorneys and the judge—not at cross purposes. "But judges can't be involved in settlement discussions," Judge Goldfarb countered. "If we have a trial we can only consider the evidence admitted at trial, not settlement discussions. We can't be a part of them."

Judge Walker mentioned psychological evaluations "as a last resort that may produce solutions I wouldn't have thought of. Although they sometimes just identify unsolvable problems and they are expensive." Judge Lopez agreed that psychological evaluations "can be helpful if they give us a point of clarity so that we can decide what tools to use to help this family." Judge Sullivan pointed out that in pro-se cases, where the parents do not have attorneys, a federally-funded program exists in Chicago that employs a case manager to "pierce through ridiculous positions the parents take and help to allocate timesharing and decision making between them." It is a very good program and a big help to the judges, but it is only for cases without attorneys, she said.

Other tools the judges found helpful were parenting classes, Salvation Army programs to teach dads to be dads, early mediation, parent coordinators and of course guardians ad litem. Judge Sullivan mentioned social services workers located across from the courthouse that were available for three sessions for parents in family law cases. The cost associated with these tools, particularly parent coordination, psychological evaluations and collaborative divorce, was a big obstacle to many parents. It would be wonderful if all complicated divorces were handled collaboratively, the judges agreed, but the expense is prohibitive and only the wealthiest of litigants can afford it.

Judge Bowes ended the session by praising guardians ad litem. "Parents will want to get the guardians on their side. But it is good practice, as they do the same with the judge. Each parent wants the judge on their side." Mr. Wessel, who as a guardian ad litem, often meets together with the parents as a quasi-mediator to help them fashion a parenting plan. "I assure their lawyers that nothing will be signed, but if I can get them to focus and learn what their agendas are—maybe dad wants to reconcile but mom's agenda is just economic—it becomes clear which cases will have to go to trial."

Bob Ackley, a friend, lawyer and guardian ad litem from Lake County north of Chicago, filled us in on "what works" in his cases as he kindly drove us to the airport after our session in the courtroom. Bob emphasized that, "Children do better when they have a good relationship with both parents.

"Children will thrive when their parents have a good coparenting relationship. If parents are unable to co-parent, they must work together as co-workers in raising their child. The relationship may be over, but the family continues. Teamwork is essential. Failing a good coparenting relationship, the parents at least must establish a good working relationship. In an employment setting, they would be fired for treating a co-worker the way the treat their co-parent!

"Focus on the child's needs, not the parent's needs. Rules, routines, discipline and schedules are not just for children. Be responsible, be responsive and be respectful."

Bob proclaimed that lunch with the judges was successful. When we left the courtroom one judge was overheard saying "This was much better than I thought it would be."

Chapter 33
Listening

"Listening" is the very first chapter in the fine book, *How To Communicate: The Ultimate Guide on Improving Your Personal and Professional Relationships.* It is easy to see why the authors, Matthew McKay, Martha Davis and Patrick Fanning, gave "Listening" such high priority. The ability to listen—fully, openly and completely—to another person absolutely strengthens the relationship.

But why would you want to improve a relationship that has ended? Because it hasn't ended, if you have a child together. It is a relationship between co-parents that needs to be as good as possible for the best interest of the child.

Most co-parents find speaking much easier than listening. There's a reason for that. Co-parents often want to be *first. First* to speak, to text or to send an e mail. *First* seems like taking control, playing offense. Whoever gets the first word in wins, right? Co-parents may view listening as passive as well as scary because they've lost control when the other parent is talking. What will they say? Do I want to hear this? How will I respond? That is how moms and dads think, especially when real coparenting communication has broken down. Yet effective listening can be a weapon as well as a shield because real listening elicits information. Knowledge is power.

Close friends listen easily to each other. They know that as they confide in one another, friendships deepen. True friends know that it can be dangerous not to listen. They will miss important details. Their advice will be inadequate. Co-parents usually aren't close friends but listening skills are even more important.

Let's look at two real coparenting situations we've experienced.

1. Josh and Adrienne hold high-level positions in a health-care provider. They regard themselves as excellent communicators with the staffs they supervise. They ignored company rules to get romantically involved

with each other. They broke up two months later after advice from their supervisors. A month later Adrienne told Jack she was pregnant. Both in their mid-thirties, this is the first child for each. Initially Josh wanted Adrienne to abort their child; however, a week later he changed his mind and tearfully told her he wanted to be a father. They are excited about the baby but unsure how they can co-parent. They hardly know each other outside of work. They know they will have to talk to each other about the child, but they don't know how. They meet over coffee during the pregnancy to discuss the future.

Josh jumps in first: "You'll be happy to know I'm taking a parenting class on newborns and toddlers. I want to be a father to our child right from the start, maybe having the baby every other week…I learned that you can pump breast milk and…" Adrienne interrupts: "What the hell are you talking about? You wanted an abortion and now you think a couple of parenting classes makes you an expert on raising a newborn, a newborn who needs a mother and…." Josh cuts in, shouting over her "you didn't create this baby by yourself, he's half me and the instructor said every child needs both parents because…" Adrienne stands up, leaning over Josh, "But not in the beginning when a baby needs to bond with his mother." She turns and leaves without another word.

It's easy to see that Josh and Adrienne care deeply about this issue but each wants to talk, to be first to get their point across. Real listening isn't happening. The emotional conversation breaks down. If Josh and Adrienne had set some ground rules first, the conversation might have been more constructive. Ground rules could include: 1. We are here to try to understand each other. 2. Our baby is the most important person in this conversation. 3. We are willing to learn something about each other. 4. Not everything has to be decided now. 5. We will go home, think things over and meet again.

2. Tammy and Chip have been divorced for five years, since their twins were six years old. Coparenting went quite well as the twins attended an elementary school that both Tammy and Chip liked and supported. Next year's transition into middle school has created problems for the family. Tammy and Chip have different ideas for a school and the twins themselves don't like either choice. When they meet to discuss the issue, Tammy announces that she's ready "to hear you on why you want that

school, but only if you show me its ranking and state-wide test scores." Chip pretends to Google test scores on his I Phone, knowing they are not available, while preparing his real argument. Tammy knows he is stalling, and decides to lay out, point by point, her argument for the middle school she likes. Chip puts his phone down and nods robotically at each point she makes. When she finishes, he responds, "The twins have entirely different ideas themselves." Tammy throws her hands in the air. Chip asks "What did I do wrong?"

Tammy and Chip are engaged in pseudo-listening, not real listening. Tammy begins by asking for one specific piece of information and ignoring everything else. Chip's response is to fiddle with his phone, buying time to prepare his response. Tammy takes advantage of the silence to deliver her entire argument. Chip half-listens and then changes the subject, ending the conversation. Both Tammy and Chip are pseudo listeners as neither is wanting or intending to really listen to the other.

The authors of *How to Communicate* list the typical needs met by pseudo-listening as follows:

1. Making people think you are interested so they will like you.
2. Being alert to see if you are in danger of being rejected.
3. Listening for one specific piece of information and ignoring everything else.
4. Buying time to prepare your next comment.
5. Half-listening so someone will listen to you.
6. Listening to find someone's vulnerabilities or to take advantage.
7. Looking for the weak points in an argument so you can always be right, listening to get ammunition for attack.
8. Checking to see how people are reacting, making sure you produce the desired effect.
9. Half-listening because a good, kind, or nice person would.
10. Half-listening because you don't know how to get away without hurting or offending someone.

Before you have those difficult conversations with your co-parent, you should review what your different goals are and what it would take to understand the competing goals. Role playing with a friend could be helpful. The essence of real listening will come easily if you sincerely want to hear what is being said. Did you hear that? That's important! You must *sincerely* want to hear what is being said. But watch out for the roadblocks!

In *How To Communicate,* the authors list twelve roadblocks to real listening. They are: comparing, mind reading, rehearsing, filtering, judging, dreaming, identifying, advising, sparing, being right, derailing and placating. It easy to see how any of these roadblocks get in the way of real listening.

Let's look for roadblocks to listening in another real coparenting case:

Lisa and Todd are recently separated parents of two very busy teenagers. Their son plays soccer for his high school and for a competitive league. Their daughter is a talented gymnast. Both children have tough practice schedules and a lot of homework. Lisa and Todd both want to work things out between themselves, mostly to avoid the high costs of divorce attorneys.

When the therapist first met Lisa, he couldn't believe how fast she talked. He could hardly get a word in sideways. One sentence ran into another as she poured out her ideas for timesharing, division of assets, child support and the sale of the marital home. All in one breath, it seemed. Todd said that is how she came across to him when they tried to resolve things. She didn't pause, and he didn't participate. Obviously, there was no agreement. Their family therapist said that Lisa had rehearsed her position so often, and was so sure that she was right, that she sabotaged any real discussion with Todd before it got started. She assumed she knew his response. She was afraid to hear it. The faster Lisa spoke, the less opportunity Todd had to weigh in with his ideas. She never gave him a chance.

The roadblocks Lisa put up are obvious: mind reading, rehearsing, being right and derailing the discussion.

To practice identifying roadblocks, look back and examine recent difficult conversations you have had with a friend, fellow employee or in a professional or personal relationship. As you replay the conversations, try to identify the roadblocks *each of you* brought to the table that impaired real listening. If you are coparenting, suggest having a conversation just to discuss roadblocks. And be ready to actively listen!

On a personal note, I, Irene, always thought I was a good listener because I am an experienced lawyer. Wrong! In marriage counseling sessions a few years ago, I discovered I was not a good listener because I was too good at rehearsing, filtering, judging, advising, sparring and being right.

We can all learn to be better listeners.

Chapter 34
Apologies: Why They Beat the "Damnit Doll"

In *Mistakes Were Made (but not by me),* authors Carol Tavris and Elliot Aronson discuss venting, how it can backfire and fuel the need to justify what *you* said or did that might be actually wrong.

"Feeling stressed? One Internet Source teaches you how to make your own little Dammit Doll, which 'can be thrown, jabbed, stomped and even strangled 'til all the frustration leaves you.' A little poem goes with it:

- → "Whenever things don't go so well,
- → And you want to hit the wall and yell,
- → Here's a little dammit doll that you can't do without.
- → Just grasp it firmly by the legs and find a place to slam it.
- → And as you whack the stuffing out, yell, "Dammit, dammit, dammit."

"The Dammit Doll reflects one of the most entrenched convictions in our culture, fostered by the psychoanalytic belief in the benefits of catharsis: expressing anger or behaving aggressively gets rid of anger. Throw that doll, hit a punching bag, shout at your spouse; you'll feel better afterward. Actually, decades of experimental research have found exactly the opposite: when people vent their feelings aggressively, they often feel worse, pump up their blood pressure, and make themselves even angrier."

Placing blame rarely puts conflict to rest. But admitting fault, even if you feel the problem is *mostly* your co-parent's doing, can be very productive in resolving conflict and rebuilding necessary trust. As we've said so often, coparenting is so different from the relationship we have with colleagues, neighbors, friends or even relatives, whose mishaps or slights we can write off, ignore or deal with later. Coparenting is a three-way street, a triangle, with the best interest of the children at the top. Let's look at apologies that way. Our children as well as our co-parent may be owed an apology.

If you are the one apologizing, be prompt, sincere and to the point. Don't try to sneak in excuses, past rebukes, or justifications for your behavior. K.I.S.S., Keep It Simple, Stupid, is good advice. "I'm sorry I…" is much more effective than a paragraph of whining about the bad day at the office you had that led to your coparenting mistake. If you are on the receiving end of an apology, it is important to take the apology at face value, not to gloat and to suppress an urge to say "I told you so" or to punish. Retaliation and punishment add fire to the conflict which burns the coparenting relationship. This is detrimental to you, your co-parent and your children. Receiving an apology magnanimously is as important as giving one.

Except for infants and toddlers, who are unable to conceptualize coparenting disputes, most children are keenly aware of the relationship between their co-parents—the people they love most in the world. Like radar, they are tuned into differences in speech volume, mean words, body gestures and signs of frustration. Children learn to be flexible, to adjust and to respect others, at home and in school. We don't want them to learn differently from their co-parents.

Therefore, when Ashley, the mom, arbitrarily refuses to switch timesharing when dad's parents have come into town unexpectedly and want to take their grandchildren to a theme park for a day, children resent this. Likewise, when Judd, the dad insists on a long summer vacation that doesn't take into consideration schoolteacher Ashley's limited time with the children, the children resent this. If those children are old enough to be tuned into the issues, they are old enough to deserve an apology. These are big issues, so imagine the myriad of smaller issues between co-parents that deserve an apology from one to the other, many of them played out in front of the children. That's why children deserve an apology too.

"Seven Steps for Apologizing to Your Child" found on the Positive Coparenting website has the best advice I've seen for coparenting apologies that involve the child. Stay calm and be sincere, they say, and follow these seven steps:

1. Own your feelings and take responsibility for them.
2. Connect the feeling to the action.
3. Point out which action of yours was inappropriate and explain why. Your kids will learn that they can't act that way, either.
4. Acknowledge if they were hurt or scared. If your action was sparked by something your kids did or didn't do, make sure they understand that your affection is not based on them meeting your expectations.
5. Share how you plan to avoid this situation in the future.
6. Ask for forgiveness. Can be as simple as "can you forgive me?"
7. Focus on amends and solutions. Offer to discuss and work out solutions to the issue with your child.

If this advice seems exactly fitted to apologize to a child in an in-tact family, without separation/divorce issues, you are correct. Children are children, no matter. The children of Rebecca and Judd in the situations above deserve apologies for plans that were spoiled.

So, what should we remember about apologies in a coparenting relationship:

1. Positive thinking. Make it a priority.
2. Open and honest communication about your children. Make it a goal.
3. Focus on finding solutions rather than getting to the bottom of the issue.
4. Remain open minded to ideas you didn't hatch.
5. Lighten up, relieve the stress, talk about the joys of your children.

Chapter 35
Managing Your Feelings

It isn't easy! Managing feelings can be difficult for many reasons: The parents never really knew each other; they had relations but not a relationship. The breakup was awful, because of infidelity, domestic violence, financial mismanagement or other problems that create baggage and distrust. The parents have new partners who create new problems in the old relationship. Or many other reasons. Yet both parents love the child and deep down both do desire better coparenting.

There is a two-step process that works for most parents. First, separate the roles. You are no longer husband and wife or intimate partners but co-parents—a mother and father linked forever because of your child. Then, in your co-parent role, control your instincts. If you find coparenting exchanges difficult it may be because you are anticipating what your co-parent will say next, where the argument will begin, rather than letting the conversation just take place. You need to come off the tree limb and back to the trunk of the tree, engaged in a meaningful conversation, or e mail exchange, in which you listen, speak, listen again, speak again, free of *assuming* what the co-parent wants or will say.

Let's break down each of these steps.

Draw a line down the middle of a sheet of paper. On the left side, write all the personal problems you had with your ex when you were together, including communication problems. On the right side, list only those problems that involve the child. Read that list a few times, to be sure that you are thorough and focused. Then cut the left side off and discard it. Yes, it is true that a lousy spouse can be a good parent and co-parent! You need to put the personal problems with your ex aside and concentrate on those involving your child. Then, to get in the right frame of mind, you need to expand the right side of the list to include all the good points you ex has as a parent. That exercise provides needed balance.

To get back to the trunk of the tree, you need to discard or temporarily retire all the *assumptions* you have about how your co-parent will react to your suggestions, advice or even constructive criticism. Most of us think we have good instincts and can anticipate behaviors. But people change—especially after a divorce and especially after a volatile relationship. Freed of past *assumptions,* co-parents can create a new relationship based on mutual respect and the love they both have for the child they created together.

Let's take a look at two common situations.

Pam and Scott dated for a short time before she became pregnant. They got married because of the pregnancy and were divorced two months after Lori's birth. Both parents harbor a lot of guilt: Pam because she told Scott she was using birth control, and Scott because of the divorce that he alone wanted. Their coparenting conversations begin abruptly and end in anger. Pam complains that Scott interrupts her, cuts her off, never listens to her which was what he did while they were dating. Scott complains that Pam would not let him get a word in edgewise, talking over him all the time, and that was why he wanted to divorce. In coparenting counseling, both admitted to causing the problem. Scott said he had to interrupt because Pam would "run her mouth nonstop and I assumed I wouldn't have a chance to speak." Pam said she would "talk quickly and get in all I wanted because I assumed he would interrupt me." The therapist brought both of them back to the trunk of the tree. Free of assumptions, Pam and Scott began to have meaningful conversations about their daughter.

Walt and Rosemary had a ten-year marriage that dissolved when they grew apart pursuing different careers. Their two children were fortunate as the family had enjoyed a month of summer vacation each year in Maine at Rosemary's family home. The parents agreed to a 50/50, week on/week off timesharing schedule but Rosemary was afraid to bring up summer vacation as she assumed Walt would object to the children having a month in Maine with her family. When Rosemary did not mention Maine in the negotiations, Walt assumed she was willing to carry the 50/50 timesharing schedule through the summer. When Rosemary announced in June that she had made airline reservations for the next month, Walt erupted, saying he had made vacation plans based on the existing schedule. Both avoided talking about it during the negotiations, so this was a case of avoidance as well as assumptions. It turned out that Walt did not really object to the month in Maine. He thought it was a great opportunity for the children each summer. He just wanted to know well enough in advance to be able to plan his own vacation with the children.

So, give it a try. Make the two lists, then add the good points to the list about parenting. Next, put away past assumptions and try to experience a conversation or e mail exchange that flows, without anticipating what the other parent may say or do. It can be an eye-opening experience, as the exchange flows naturally and can lead to unexpected area of agreement and new respect. Scary at first, maybe, but a bold step to managing your feelings and better coparenting.

Chapter 36
Parallel Parenting

Co-parents who struggle with coparenting sometimes turn to "parallel parenting," either intentionally or by happenstance. It is an alternative to coparenting, recommended by some therapists and even family law judges where the parents are in extremely high conflict, unable to communicate or to stop sparring and fighting with each other.

Picture parallel lines running across a page until a child reaches majority, usually 18 years old. In between those lines, like "W's" is the child rotating between the parents Each parent sets the child's activities, household rules, homework requirements, playmates and friends, during that parent's timesharing. Parallel parenting requires a detailed parenting plan with little need for flexibility as the goal is to minimize contact between the parents.

Parallel parenting may be a relief for parents caught in domestic violence or mental health situations with a co-parent. It may be helpful in long distance coparenting, where the child lives with one parent during the school year and the other parent during school holidays and summer vacation. But too often parallel parenting is a lazy way out of true coparenting, where the focus is the best interest of the child.

Let's look at the pros and cons: For a very young child or toddler, parallel parenting may seem to work because there are no school or extra-curricular issues, no major discipline problems, cell phone or social media concerns, curfews or friends who are "bad influences." It may seem kind of easy to parallel parent. But as the child enters school and sports teams, band or theatre practice, making friends on his own and knowing more about electronics than either parent, parallel parenting fails. In fact, it often leads to manipulation by the child, who pits one parent against the other just trying to get their needs met, favoring the more liberal parent in matters of discipline, cell phone use, curfew or even homework. Parents need to be on the same page in these matters. It's obvious that the child can't attend two different schools at the same time or join soccer and basketball teams that have the same schedules. Co-parents need to agree and get help to do so if coparenting continues to be conflictual.

It's obvious that the parent who tries to bribe the child with lax rules regarding chores, curfew, homework, friends, social media and/or cell phone use does a disservice to the co-parent. However, that behavior is also very detrimental to the child, who quickly learns that rules don't matter at least in one household. Major trouble lies ahead for that child.

Intact families often have parents who disagree on children's issues. However, because they live together, they often compromise, or split the responsibilities. If manipulation occurs, it can be cut off quickly. The focus of coparenting is on the best interest of the child. It's not who "won" the argument this time. Coparenting requires good communication, compromise, principled negotiation, flexibility, creativity, a willingness to seek help when needed and always, always a laser focus on the child.

Parallel parenting is a poor substitute for effective coparenting that keeps the child at the center and is aimed at being in the best interest of the child. There are few ways to successfully manage children's complex emotions and needs while co-parents continue to ignore everything but their own feelings and needs. The focus should always be on the child and what they need.

Working with a Parent Coordinator can help reduce ongoing conflict over important parenting decisions, but it doesn't address the residual pain and loss for the child who continues to see his parents fighting, ignoring, and being spiteful. Children who are pulled into the middle of the conflict suffer great emotional harm. This harm is detrimental to their development, their mental health, physical health and the relationships that sustain children throughout their childhoods. Those relationships, primarily with their parents and those responsible for their nurturing and care are seriously injured by the conflict the child sees and feels around them.

The parent-child relationship is the most important and sustaining relationship of a child's life. The safety, security, and unconditional love that a child experiences in a healthy parent-child relationship sets the foundation for healthy development and for positive and secure relationship throughout that child's life. When this relationship is negatively impacted by witnessing conflict between two beloved parents, the child's life is changed forever.

How co-parents navigate their coparenting relationship sets the emotional tone for their relationship with their child. Every negative interaction that a child must witness or experience between their parents is an injury to the parent-child relationship. When children are hurt repeatedly by their parents, they build up emotional walls to the connection that they need, creating emotional distance and alienation. At some point, the parent-child relationship is so injured that parents can no longer provide the emotional support that their child needs to weather the road of life. Sadly, this leaves both parent and child suffering and struggling to reconnect. The best chance for healing is a change in the coparenting environment and a major relationship repair with a skilled counselor. Run, don't walk, to a professional to help protect your child from your high-conflict coparenting relationship. Do it for you, but mostly, do it for your children and the relationship that they deserve to have with you.

Part V
Collaborative Divorce*

---

* If you have read this far in the book, you may be shaking your head, tearing at your hair or screaming out loud:
"There MUST be a better way!"
There is, and it is called COLLABORATIVE DIVORCE

Chapter 37
What Is Collaborative Divorce?

Collaborative divorce recognizes that parenting relationships and obligations continue even when a marriage ends if children are involved. The process allows the parents to reach agreements that focus on their most important individual and family goals and, of course, the best interest of their children. The parents and even extended family members learn to move forward in a positive, child-centered manner, focused on the future rather than dwelling on the wounds, disputes and blame of the past. Each person impacted by the divorce—especially the children—will have the best post-divorce lives possible without the damage of a highly litigated separation and divorce. The process can work in paternity cases as well.

The general principles of the collaborative divorce process are these:

1. It is contractual. The parents and their attorneys sign a contract promising to try to settle all of the issues outside of court and without threatening to go to court.
2. Parents retain control. Instead of handing control to a judge who has little time or familiarity with the family's circumstances, parents retain control by working with specially trained professionals to arrive at solutions that fit them as individuals and as a family.
3. Scheduling is flexible and parent friendly. Instead of being governed by a court or litigation schedule, meetings with the parents and collaborative team members are scheduled based on convenience for all participants.
4. It is a team effort. Costs are reduced by using agreed-upon instead of competing experts. The lawyers for each parent are trained in the

collaborative process and commit not to take the case into litigation if the collaborative effort fails.
5. It is still a private, confidential process. Each parent can have confidential conversations with their attorney and arrive at a strategy to achieve goals confidentially. The setting is an office rather than a courtroom.

If you wonder why parents who are so agreeable and work together so well even bother to get divorced, you are not alone. It is a common question. However, in our highly mobile, fluid, every-changing society, with parents moving in an out of different jobs and educational goals while their children are expressing different needs as they mature, it is not unusual for parents to grow apart without animosity or high conflict. These are the parents most suited for collaborative divorce; however, a good collaborative team can work through hurt, betrayal and conflict.

The well-trained professionals in the collaborative divorce field will say they succeed with higher conflict cases because the initial act of signing a contract for a collaborative process reduces conflict from the beginning. This is true. Through training, attorneys will quickly realize the cases that cannot be handled collaboratively. Those are the cases with significant mental health issues for one or both parents, domestic violence with power and control issues or severe parental alienation which has significantly altered the relationship between one of the parents and the children.

Collaborative divorce may not be for everyone, but when it works, thousands of dollars spent on litigation can be saved for a new start for a parent or college for the kids—with a more harmonious coparenting relationship going forward. Both parents can enjoy those high school and college graduations, weddings and grandchildren which will come sooner than expected.

The next few chapters should help you analyze whether collaborative divorce is best for you, your loved ones, your clients or patients.

Chapter 38
The Collaborative Team

Teamwork is the engine that drives the collaborative divorce process to a successful resolution—a settlement agreement and parenting plan that the judge can sign off on after congratulating everyone involved.

Divorce and child custody/timesharing litigation does not have to be a knock down, War of the Roses battle. Collaboration begins with skilled attorneys trained in the process and parents willing to shove aside past wounds and grievances to negotiate in good faith for a resolution that is in the best interest of the child.

Family lawyers receive training from local, state and even international organizations, such as the Tampa Bay Academy of Collaborative Professionals (TBACP), the Florida Academy of Collaborative Professionals (FACP) or the International Academy of Collaborative Professionals (IACP). All have websites filled with information about its members, training schedules and the process in general.

Collaborative divorce lawyers are generally well-known family law practitioners of skill and integrity who can be trusted to negotiate in good faith and with full disclosure. The lawyers are trained in the collaborative methodology and understand what is happening each step of the way towards a successful resolution. Privacy is still important. The parties can discuss issues of importance to them and their children with their lawyers in confidence.

If a parent demonstrates frustration, anger or fear of communicating, a neutral communications facilitator can be a wise and helpful addition to the team. This is usually an experienced mental health professional or divorce counselor who works with the parents separately or in the group meetings to help them communicate better during the process and after the divorce.

Team members may include an accountant, business evaluator or employment specialist, depending on the issues in the case. The big difference with the collaborative process is that the team agrees to use one expert in each field, saving litigation costs and the need to challenge an opposing expert's credentials. This is a huge advantage of collaboration as it sets the tone for future agreements which should lead to a full resolution of all issues. Good collaborative lawyers boast of successful settlements in 95% of their cases.

Chapter 39
Two Lawyers Share Their Experiences

Nancy Harris and Lee Greene are pioneers in collaborative divorce law in the Tampa Bay area of Florida.

Nancy states that training in collaboration "has changed the way conflict is resolved through the world, and not just in divorce cases."

"It starts with the initial petition," Nancy said. "The parties have to agree to a 'participation agreement.' If differences aren't resolved, the attorneys must withdraw from the case. This creates a safe sanctuary for the parties and lawyers to work together. No one gains from not settling the case.

"You can see the process working right in front of you. The parents come in not talking to each other about parenting issues and in a while, they are problem solving and working out a parenting plan that fits their needs. Even if there are allegations of abuse, an evaluator can be part of the team and that evaluator can still testify in court if necessary.

"The collaborative process eliminates so much post-dissolution litigation," she added. "It gives the parties techniques to problem solve themselves. That's worth so much."

Lee Greene finds the process "absolutely terrific because of the process itself. The benefit to the children is obvious because the process creates a plan for better communicating and better coparenting that is long lasting.

"First, you lower them temperature. Then you identify your goals. Next you build off on where there is a communality. For example, no parent will say they do not act in the best interest of their children. The negotiations then become family-oriented rather than self-oriented and the transition to a new kind of family is less hurtful. It is a new definition of family."

Lee gave examples of how creative the process could be compared to the limitations placed on the judge. "Alimony, child support, private school tuition can all be negotiated totally to maximize the cash flow…something a judge can't do. The parents retain control of the process and the future, rather than taking a chance in court."

Both Nancy and Lee value the participation of the mental health professional, often as the team leader. "The cases still are emotional, especially at the beginning, so the mental health professional meets with the whole team first and then with each parent to develop a parenting plan," Nancy said. "A parent is less likely to think the other lawyer is getting a step up on them." Lee added that "the mental health professionals look for 'trigger points' if things begin to get hostile. They have the expertise to identify those points and to resolve them."

Collaborative divorce is not cheap. The team members are well paid. However, compared to the expense of on-going litigation, document discovery, depositions, the cost of experts thought to be "hired guns" for each side, and endless hearings, the collaborative process can actually save money. Without a doubt the children benefit tremendously as their parents learn to co-parent respectfully and cooperatively in their new family.

Chapter 40
The Mental Health Professional

Dr Kim E. Costello, a therapist and founder of the Costello Center in St. Petersburg, Fl., often serves as the neutral mental health facilitator. She said that "collaborative divorce has completely changed my work. I have seen a transformation with couples who may come in angry and with a list of concerns but quickly work for the best interest of the children, due to the process itself. Their children are not going to be those who grow up while their parents spend most of the time fighting each other. Parents learn to love their children more than they hate each other."

Dr Costello said that only a handful of the many collaborative cases she has worked on are unsuccessful. "Cases with substance abuse or a lot of infidelity are difficult, but they can be handled collaboratively. The parents are taught to communicate and to work through things at the beginning of the proceedings. Litigation certainly does not provide this skill set.

"Children do better when they have a good relationship with both parents. Children of divorce can thrive when their parents have a good coparenting relationship. The marital relationship is over, but the family continues. Teamwork is essential, and the collaborative process builds that concept of teamwork from the beginning."

In addition to leading collaborative teams, Dr Costello provides individual therapy and parent coordination to divorcing couples. "When I see poor coparenting," she said, "I often use the example of a co-worker. You would not treat a co-worker the way you are treating your co-parent. You have to focus on your child's needs, not your own. Rules, routine, discipline and schedules are not just for children. Be responsible, responsive and respectful."

Dr Costello lists the various roles she serves when acting as the neutral mental health professional on the collaborative team. She is an advisor, a mediator, a guide, a supporter and a facilitator.

Chapter 41
View from the Bench

Chief Family Law Judge Jack Helinger cares about families. It shows front and center in his St. Petersburg, Florida, courtroom. He has chosen to preside over family law cases when his seniority would allow him to move to any other division in the courthouse. He treats each family law case individually. He is not shy about giving advice to the parents and attorneys at case management conferences or pre-trial hearings when everyone is seeking a contested final hearing, especially one involving children.

"If you think things are bad now," he warns them, "they will only get worse after a final hearing that will cost you both thousands of dollars and polarize the relationship as each side attacks the other's character, credibility and parenting skills. Then, following this battle, we expect mom and dad to leave the courtroom and to co-parent amicably in the best interest of their children. It is too much to ask. It will get worse, not better, and folks may be in and out of court forever. What a crazy system!

"I've tried for years to think of a better solution than contested family law matters—especially those involving children. I've wrestled with the issue more than any in my judicial career. The only solution I can think of is: Don't Do It!

"Find some compromise, some middle ground, *some* point of agreement. You know your children. I don't. Yet you expect me to listen to the disputed facts, the various therapists, apply the law and make a ruling that affects you and your children for years to come. I'll be glad to do it, because that's what I'm paid to do. But I barely know you two and I've never met your children.

"Doesn't it make good sense for the two of you—assisted by your lawyers, the parent coordinator, the family therapists and the guardian ad litem—to reach a decision that is in the best interest of the children you love so much?

Doesn't it? "

Chapter 42
Non-Violent Communication (NVC)

Marshall B. Rosenberg, PhD, is the founder of a movement that stresses empathy, collaboration, authenticity and freedom "as a way of communicating that leads us to give from the heart."

Frankly, we don't like the word "nonviolent," and neither does Dr Kim Costello, a collaborative divorce team leader. The alternative meaning is "compassionate communication" and that is the process Dr Rosenberg, now deceased, describes in the extremely helpful book he wrote in 2015 as a guide to "a language of life, a way of communicating that leads us to give from the heart."

Dr Rosenberg's teachings have been used to reduce violence in prisons, to mediate disputes between long standing enemies in the Mideast, and in workplace situations where conflict resolution is essential. "We perceive relationships in a new light when we use NVC to hear our own deeper needs and those of others," Dr Rosenberg wrote.

There is so much helpful information in Dr Rosenberg's way of communicating that could be useful to co-parents struggling with communication issues, including power and control and imbalance in their relationship. We particularly like the chapters about taking responsibility for our feelings and receiving empathically. Dr Rosenberg defines empathy as "emptying our mind and listening with our whole being." What an inspiring instruction for co-parents, whose "whole beings" were once merged to create the child or children they love so much.

The entire book, *Nonviolent Communication,* is so helpful to co-parents. It doesn't do justice to quote sparingly from it; however, in the chapter summarizing empathy, Dr Rosenberg states:

"Empathy is a respectful understanding of what others are experiencing. We often have a strong urge to give advice or reassurance or to explain our own position or feeling. Empathy, however, causes upon us to empty our mind and listen to others with our whole being.

"In NVC, no matter what words others may use to express themselves, we simply listen for their observations, feelings, needs and requests. Then we may wish to reflect back, paraphrasing what we have understood. We stay with empathy and allow others the opportunity to fully express themselves before we turn our attention to solutions or requests for relief.

"We need empathy to give empathy. When we sense ourselves being defensive or unable to empathize, we need to (1) stop, breathe, give ourselves empathy; (2) scream non-violently; or (3) take time out."

We wish you better, improved "nonviolent" coparenting as you learn to develop more empathy for yourselves and your co-parents.

Marshall Rosenberg focuses on three aspects of Nonviolent communication (NVC). These components include self-empathy being a deep and compassionate awareness of one's own inner experience, empathy based on understanding and sharing emotions expressed by others, and honest self-expression which allows us to express ourselves authentically in a way that is likely to inspire compassion in others.

Nonviolent communication is rooted in the ideology that all human beings have the capacity for compassion and only fall back on behavior that harms others when they do not have the ability to recognize and utilize more effective strategies for meeting needs. We must travel our own road to self-growth by becoming observers of our behavior and others, receiving and expressing feelings, stating our needs clearly and making our requests fairly.

There are so many helpful thoughts and ideas in *Nonviolent Communication*. If we were to ascribe to embracing changes in our communication, we could transform our relationships and our lives. Dr Rosenberg emphasizes critical points in understanding how we are impacted by our thoughts and expectations. If we can reflect on our own patterns of negative thinking and look at our patterns of negative communication, we can then choose to think differently and respond differently. It is in these changes that we choose to make where we open the doors to experiencing more joy in life, for ourselves, for others, and for our children. He emphasizes that we need to do things by feeling the pure joy of experiencing life.

Dr Rosenberg emphasizes attending to our own communication and how it expresses our needs in ways that others can receive. We must be able to express what is alive in us by letting others know what is meeting our needs or not meeting our needs. We can also make clear observations of other people's actions without mixing in any evaluations. Keeping observation and evaluation separate in our communication is important in order to communicate to have our needs met, which is the reason for communication in general. Less judgement, more compassion, sets the stage for changes in the emotional tone of our relationships.

In "non-violent communication", or "compassionate communication", we must think deeply about our own behavior first. Changing our strategies for communication quite often changes the ways that others communicate with us. Co-parents must agree to work on communication issues which are negatively impacting the coparenting relationship and agree that they are able to practice patience, kindness, and compassion for the sake of their children and for their own pursuit of happiness and joy.

Chapter 43
Last Words... Lighten Up...
Laugh a Lot... And Love, Love, Love

Coparenting anxiety can seem so exhausting that it is easy to forget all the good things about these beautiful children the two of you created who turn into adolescents, teenagers and young adults in the blink of an eye. Overall, because of the children, there is more fun than frustration, more happiness than heartache and more peace than there are problems. Co-parents need to lighten up, laugh a lot at the antics of their children, laugh with their children and love them...love them...love them. Tell them often how much you love them, as they really do love you, right from their infancy. Love for their parents is built into them, even as tired toddlers, angry adolescents or troubled teenagers.

In that light, a group of 4 to 10-year-olds was asked, "What does love mean?" Here's a selection of their wise and wonderful replies...from the mouths of babes!

"When someone loves you, the way they say your name is different. You just know that your name is safe in their mouth." (Billy-age 7)

"Love is sharing even if you think you don't have enough." (Chrissie-age 6)

"Love is like medicine and hate is like poison. If everybody knew that we'd all be happy." (Keisha-age 8)

"Love is the quiet sound in the room when the people you care about are all together." (Luis-age 10)

"My mommy said they adopted me because they wanted one more way to grow love in our family. She said I grew in her heart, not in her belly." (Hector-age 9)

"Love is when you tell a boy you like his shirt, and then he wears it every day." (Noelle-age 7)

"During my piano recital, I was on a stage and I was scared. I looked at all the people watching me, and I saw my daddy waving and smiling. I wasn't scared anymore. Love does that." (Cindy-age 8)

"Love is what makes you smile when you're too tired to think." (Terri-age 9)

You, dear reader, may be way too tired to think after finishing this book, so just smile and love them all!

Epilogue

By: Florida Circuit Court Judge Jack Helinger

You have now read about families, their challenges, and their pathways to good parenting relations. Let's look at three pairs of parents, how they handled their situations, and the ultimate effect on their children.

1) One couple had good reason to be angry at each other. The husband could not control his anger and too often took it out on the wife and children. The wife became infatuated with a co-worker who treated her kindly and had an affair with him. The husband blew up when he found out, resulting in a Domestic Violence Injunction and removal from the house.

Both blamed the other. Neither accepted any responsibility for their actions. The children began acting out in school and home. The judge realized early in the case that both parents contributed to the problems and tried to administer therapeutic justice. The parents resisted. Both stayed in the anger phase. Both resisted the help of the Court ordered Parent Coordinator. Both said the children were fine (they weren't) and stopped taking them to counseling. After a contested final hearing, the Court was left with no option other than making a very structured, specific, parenting plan and ordering strict compliance. Both parents continued to bad mouth the other parent to anyone who would listen—including the children.

Let's see how the children are doing when the son is 22 and the daughter is 20. The mother had the son removed from her home when he turned 18 in his senior year for hitting her and keeping drugs in the house. He dropped out of high school four months before graduation. He briefly moved into his father's home but their similar personalities did not mesh. He has been on probation for drug possession and battery. He has little relationship with either parent. Their daughter lives with her boyfriend and their one-year-old daughter. She is a cashier making minimum wage.

2) Bob and Sue were high school sweethearts, married at 20, and had children at 23 and 25. They loved each other and planned to grow old together, enjoying grandchildren. Unfortunately, the pressure of jobs, lack of money, and child demands led them to grow apart. After staying together "for the kids," they decided to divorce when the children were 12 and 10. At first, they handled the separation well, but as soon as each other started to date, problems started. Each found problems with the new paramours. Each did not want the children around the new boyfriend/girlfriend. Each started living with the new partner before the divorce was completed. The communication and respect diminished. The conflict rose.

The Court tried to help the parties develop to a better state, but both parties refused. The children were affected by the battles and prodding for information by both parents. The parents decided the Court had to decide their children's futures. The final hearing primarily was each side saying derogatory things about the other and the new partners.

The judge did her best and entered a final judgement and parenting plan. The judge ordered counseling for everyone. No one was pleased with the decision, and resisted counseling.

The battles and blame games continued for the next eight years. The children took turns refusing to go to the other parent's home when things didn't go their way. The parents periodically were back in Court on Motions for Contempt on Supplemental Petitions to Modify. These bright children did not do well in school. Both children moved from their home area in their early 20s. Both children have limited/guarded relationships with their parents.

3) The parents met and started dating in their senior years of college. Three years later they married. They both had jobs in their given career fields. Two years later they had their daughter and four years later, their son. They were the typical functioning family. Both parents started to have a cocktail every evening to "wind down." One became two, and soon two became four. Arguments ensued. The children saw the drinking and heard the arguments. One night, the drinking got out of hand and the police were called. The children witnessed everything.

A divorce was soon filed. The divorce and separation did not help the anger and alcohol abuse. In a Motion for Temporary Time Sharing, a wise Judge listened. The Judge's impressions: two good people who loved their children, both hard working, both caught up in the rat race of raising active children, both turned to alcohol to "unwind," both lost their ability to control their emotions (and tongues) while under the influence, both forgot about the good qualities in each other, and both did not comprehend the damage they were doing to their children.

The judge posed the question: "Do you want to continue to fight and I'll decide everything, or do you want the Court system to help you all get to a much better place?" The judge explained the unintentional damage the parents were both doing to their children.

The judge gave the parents some time to contemplate. When they returned to the Courtroom, they both said "what can you do to help us?" Instead of a contested hearing, the judge and parents (and attorneys) spent the rest of the time agreeing to a Parent Coordinator, counseling for the children, attending AA meetings, and recommending some great parenting books.

Recently, the father proudly walked their daughter down the aisle to marry the man of her dreams who she met in graduate school. Dad and his spouse sat in the same pew as mom and her new spouse. Their son was the best man for his new brother-in-law. The wedding toasts by everyone were about love and family.

You can determine which of these three scenarios you will follow. You will be the biggest influence on how your children enter adulthood.

Marriage is not easy. Divorce is painful. There is nothing harder or more important in life than being the good parent we want to be. But we often need help. You are not alone. Your circumstances are not unique. Help is available, if you accept it. Your children will be the primary beneficiaries.

Special Section: Coparenting During Covid-19 and Other Crises

Parents continuously face the challenges that society brings. These challenges can be overwhelming and greatly change our ways of life, our ways of work, and our ways of parenting. The Novel Coronavirus has impacted every human being on our planet and will continue to do so for another generation. COVID-19 has impacted every family and thus every child to some extent. Our communities have shut down, adapted new rules, closed vital services and are stretched over school closings, child-care shortages, health care crisis, and financial catastrophes at the family, community and national level.

Growing inequities in health care, education, employment opportunities and housing have created not only challenges for our families but public health issues that impact our societal functioning. During COVID-19 families have had employment disruptions with consequences around meeting basic needs including having access to affordable child-care, paying rent, getting adequate food, medicine, health care and essential items.

Many families face multiple challenges in parenting and coparenting during COVID-19. These challenges can be life changing for families. They include facing school and child-care closures requiring parents to make critical decisions over childcare and schooling issues. Considering the high cost of care for children of all ages, COVID-19 has brought costly and complicated issues for co-parents to deal with. When you layer in educational disruption and multiple transitions in care for babies and young children, this pandemic is requiring parents to find new ways of balancing work issues with the care and educational needs of their children.

Job loss stemming from quarantine has created family crisis nationwide. Many parents have been laid off, furloughed or otherwise lost work, or changed their schedules. Parents have had to adapt to a new way of working from home or on alternating work schedules. This creates complications for all parents but even more for co-parents who are timesharing and arranging visitation schedules around employment.

Sheltering in place due to exposure to COVID-19 or mandatory or suggested quarantines have become a problematic issue for coparenting. Levels of risk and the definition of what is acceptable risk for exposure to COVID-19 has been loosely interpreted leading to confusion about how we best keep our children, our loved ones and ourselves safe during these unprecedented times. These complicated issues need to be considered in coparenting as important decisions about schooling, safety and visitation need to be thoughtfully made to ensure that our children are both physically and emotionally safe.

Time sharing and visitation can become an issue when co-parents need additional flexibility in job hours or work locations. Essential workers have had to make multiple sacrifices to serve an ever-growing population of need with COVID-19. Many co-parents are essential workers and must work in job situations where they have high exposures to COVID-19. The complex factors of risk of exposure to COVID-19 add to an already difficult coparenting scenario for many families that cannot be easily resolved.

Coming to terms with temporarily modifying coparenting plans can be especially difficult during times of crisis. In a pandemic where we are often uncertain about what the actual facts are around the transmission of a virus, it can be a challenge to know how to keep our children and ourselves safe.

There are many potentially traumatic components to the COVID-19-19 pandemic. Fear of loved ones contracting COVID-19 and suffering or worse is an underlying toxic stressor for everyone. Many families have already lost family members, friends and neighbors. Children have lost teachers, grandparents and caregivers. The grief is palpable, and families need to come together during times of crisis. How can coparenting be different during this time to support children in the unique ways they need?

Below are some ideas to consider when you are coparenting during COVID-19 or another pandemic (hopefully not!).

- Know the science and the risks of transmission.
- Modify coparenting plans as needed to ensure both physical and emotional safety for children.

- Consider increased virtual contact with both co-parents to support the connection and relationship between parents and children.
- Discuss how to have conversations with your children about COVID-19. Children need to have their questions answered.
- Provide children with consistent messages, reassurance and support on a regular basis.
- Use common sense based in medical facts to make decisions.
- Consider engaging the advice or guidance of the child's pediatrician.
- Understand that fear—for our children, families and ourselves—can make us operate in overprotective ways. This is a response of love.
- Be empathetic to the change in life circumstances, overwhelming feelings, fear and uncertainty that exists for your children and your co-parent.

There is a bright side to coparenting during COVID-19. Both of us have experienced co-parents who have been more understanding and flexible with timesharing issues during a crisis that is clearly not the fault of either co-parent. Those parents put the best interest of the children first in their priorities.

Appendix, Resources

1. For the resource list:
2. https://tribecatherapy.com/coparenting-therapy/
3. Concepts that need to be considered, revised and edited from https://tribecatherapy.com/coparenting-therapy/
    1. Mistakes Were Made (but not by me): Why We Justify Foolish Beliefs, Bad Decisions, and Hurtful Acts By Carol Tavris and Elliot Aronson Mariner Books, 2007, 2015
    2. Coparenting with a Toxic Ex : What to Do When Your Ex-Spouse Tries to Turn the Kids Against You By Amy J.L. Baker, PhD and Paul R. Fine, LCSW, New Harbinger Publications, 2014
    3. The Deepest Well: Healing the Long-Term Effects of Childhood Adversity by Nadine Burke Harris, M.D. Houghton Mifflin Harcourt, 2018
    4. How To Communicate: The Ultimate Guide to Improving Your Personal and Professional Relationships by Matthew McKay, Ph.D., Martha Davis, Ph.D. and Patrick Fanning, MJF Books, 1995
    5. We Need To Talk: How To Have Conversations That Matter by Celeste Headlee, Harper Collins, 2017
    6. Difficult Conversations: How To Discuss What Matters Most by Douglas Stone, Bruce Patton and Sheila Heen of the Harvard Negotiation Project, Penguin Books, 1999
    7. Overcoming the Coparenting Trap: Essential Parenting Skills When a Child Resists a Parent by John A. Moran, Ph.D., Tyler Sullivan, and Matthew Sullivan, Ph.D., Overcoming Barriers, Inc., 2015

8. Far From The Tree: Parents, Children, And The Search For Identity by Andrew Solomon, Scribner, 2012
9. Charting the Bumpy Road of Coparenting. James McHale, Zero To Three Press, 2007
10. Coparenting: A Conceptual and Clinical Examination of Family Systems. James P. McHale, Kristin M. Lindahl, American Psychological Association, 2011
11. Young Children & Trauma. Joy Osofsky, Editor, Guildford Publications, 2004
12. Children Exposed to Violence. Margaret Mary Feerick, Gerald B. Silverman, Paul H. Brookes Pub., 2006
13. Don't Hit My Mommy!. Alicia F. Lieberman, Chandra Ghosh Ippen, and Patricia Van Horn, Zero To Three Press, 2005
14. Handbook of Infant Mental Health. Charles H. Zeanah, Editor, The Guilford Press, 2018

Biographies

Lisa S. Negrini, Ph.D., LCSW, IMHM-C

Dr Lisa S. Negrini comes to Learning Empowered as the new executive director from the University of South Florida, St. Petersburg Campus where she served as the chief operations officer of USFSP's Family Study Center and the clinical and training director at the Infant-Family Center. Dr Negrini has a doctor of philosophy in Infant and early childhood development with an emphasis in mental health and developmental disorders, a master's in social work and a bachelor's degree in psychology. Dr Negrini is also endorsed by the Florida Association of Infant Mental Health as an Infant Mental Health Mentor-Clinical (IMHM-C).

Dr Negrini brings 30 years of experience in child and family mental health, training and professional development and non-profit leadership to new role. She is a highly qualified, innovative, established leader with extensive experience and the ability to foster organizational development and expansion. Dr Negrini's specialties include providing vision for growth in non-profit agencies, executive leadership, program development, implementation, and partnership building.

Dr Negrini has decades of experience supporting programs, advocacy, research, workforce development and new initiatives for children and families. Dr Negrini has spent her career promoting integrated community systems of care for families that incorporate quality, trauma-informed services for families and community. She has developed key partnerships and collaborations across disciplines that effectively create and disseminate effective strategies and services to meet the needs of the children and their families in our community and across the state.

Dr Negrini has served on multiple non-profit Boards including serving as the President, of the Florida Association for Infant Mental Health where she facilitated state efforts to address the needs for infant and early childhood supports and services, and state-wide initiatives that address primary, secondary and tertiary prevention to promote healthy child development and support strong and resilient families.

Judge Irene Sullivan, Retired

Judge Irene Sullivan practiced trial law for 22 years in St. Petersburg, Fl., before she was elected Circuit Court Judge in 1998. She served on the juvenile and family law bench until 2011. She was an adjunct professor of juvenile law at Stetson University College of Law in Gulfport, Florida, and the author of *Raised by the Courts: One Judge's Insight into Juvenile Justice*. She travelled widely promoting juvenile justice reforms and speaking at conferences and other events.

Judge Sullivan graduated from Northwestern University's Medill School of Journalism and Stetson University College of Law. She is a board member of the Drug Free American Foundation, Inc., Ounce of Prevention of Florida, Inc., Smart Justice under Florida Tax Watch, the Pinellas County Community Foundation, "R" Club and the Center for Strategic Policy Solutions at St. Petersburg College. She was also a trustee of the Pace Center for Girls, and a board member of Pace Pinellas.

She has served on Florida's Blueprint Commission to reform juvenile justice and on statewide diversity panels. She is the recipient of many awards, including the Salvation Army's first Children's Justice Award, St. Petersburg and Clearwater Bar Association awards, the Ben C. Willard award for distinguished service from her law school, and the Ben Franklin award for statewide leadership from the St. Petersburg Tiger Bay Club. She was inducted into Stetson University's Hall of Fame in 2011 and chosen the Distinguished Alumna in 2014. In 2022 she received the advocacy award from Pace Center for Girls and was named a Woman of Distinction by the Girl Scouts of West Central Florida.

Judge Sullivan has three children, five grandchildren, one great grandchild, and three rescued cats. In addition to spending quality time with them, since her retirement from the bench in 2011 she travels, writes, teaches, consults and serves as a guardian ad litem in high conflict divorce cases.